Jack Robertson

SELLING TO THE FEDERAL GOVERNMENT

A Guide for Business

McGRAW-HILL BOOK COMPANY

New York   St. Louis   San Francisco   Auckland   Bogotá
Düsseldorf   Johannesburg   London   Madrid   Mexico
Montreal   New Delhi   Panama   Paris   São Paulo
Singapore   Sydney   Tokyo   Toronto

To my family,
my severest critics
and
my most ardent supporters

Library of Congress Cataloging in Publication Data

Robertson, Jack C
Selling to the Federal Government.

Includes index.
1. Government purchasing—United States—Handbooks,
manuals, etc. 2. Marketing—United States—Handbooks,
manuals, etc. I. Title.
JK1673.R58   658.8   78-19074
ISBN 0-07-053170-6

1234567890 DODO 7865432109

The editor for this book was W. Hodson Mogan,
the designer was Elliot Epstein, and the production supervisor
was Thomas G. Kowalczyk. It was set in Caledonia
by Bi-Comp, Incorporated.

Printed and bound by R. R. Donnelley & Sons Company.

CONTENTS

PREFACE

In 1907, in simpler days of government buying, the U.S. Army Signal Corps issued a one-page "Advertisement and Specification No. 486" for a heavier-than-air flying machine. The Wright brothers won that bid for $25,000—the first aircraft ever purchased by the government. Sixty-five years later, great changes had been wrought in both aircraft and method of procurement. The U.S. Air Force issued an 8000-page bid package—now called a Request for Proposal (RFP for short)—for a type of aircraft that was to cost more than $100 million per unit.

One might wonder whether Wilbur and Orville Wright would ever have replied to the Army if they had faced the encyclopedic, legalistic mismash of clauses, references, standards, specifications, addenda, terms, and conditions that smother the present-day RFP.

Today's government contractor has no choice. If anyone wants to do business with Uncle Sam, the RFP is almost always the process used. Yes, federal buyers still use the old-fashioned sealed bid—but less and less. Most bids, comprising 80 percent of all procurement dollars, involve some form of RFP. For better or worse, in sick contracts or in healthy ones, government procurement is married to the RFP.

This, then, is the story of the RFP and, to a lesser extent, other forms of federal procurement. From conception to ultimate contract, this is how to live with the RFP and like it. It is the world of selling to Uncle Sam.

1
WELCOME TO THE GOVERNMENT, FIRST OF THE BIG SPENDERS

1. WELCOME TO THE GOVERNMENT, FIRST OF THE BIG SPENDERS

The U.S. government is the biggest buyer in the world.

Take any commodity—the odds are that Uncle Sam buys more of it than any other government, any cartel, any multinational corporation you can name. The federal government buys 58,000 automobiles and small trucks a year—that's more vehicles than are bought annually in all but eight nations on earth. Federal bursars ordered $90 million worth of office furniture in 1977. That's enough to outfit a new office for every white-collar worker in Detroit or Houston. The government buys $75 million worth of hand tools and $73 million worth of paints and brushes a year. Government hospitals spend a quarter of a billion dollars a year on medicines. The amount of oil and gas bought each year is staggering—an estimated $3 billion worth.

You would expect Uncle Sam to be the biggest buyer of paper in the world, and he is. In fact, the General Services Administration, which orders all the government's paper, can't keep track of the more than 100 different categories of paper that are stockpiled.

The GSA maintains a catalog of 4 million different items that can be ordered by federal agencies. That's the equivalent of more than 200 regular mail-order catalogs. About 5 million tons of supplies move from GSA warehouses each year to federal agencies.

The government occupies 250 million square feet of office space in 10,000 different buildings around the country. That's slightly more space than there is in all the skyscrapers and office buildings in New York City. Just buying light bulbs and cleaning supplies for all this office space sends buying calculations soaring. Construction, decorating, maintenance, and custodial services for this federal real estate provide an estimated 18,500 contracts to industry (1977).

The federal government has 9650 computers; only ten countries have more computers installed in their entire nation. It costs more than $1 billion to run all these computers, more than it costs to operate the entire Congress.

Uncle Sam is also the biggest moviemaker in the world. The government cranks out 2000 motion pictures a year on every subject from pollution control to birth control. Federal film studios cost half a billion dollars a year—five times more than the largest studio in Hollywood.

The government buys so much merchandise that its statistics can't keep up with the torrents of orders. The best guess of GSA is that in fiscal 1977 Uncle Sam spent more than $75 billion on all industrial goods and services. That outlay alone is greater than the total economies of all but nine of the world's nations.

The $75 billion in government contracts is quickly outdated. At a 12 to 15 percent growth rate per year, by the end of the decade government contracts to industry could surpass the total U.S. government budget of only fifteen years earlier.

Few firms can ignore such a lavish market. A company president reads in the *Wall Street Journal* that an arch-competitor has snagged a big contract from the government and calls the marketing staff in on the executive carpet to explain why this company is not getting a cut of federal business. Another firm sees the staggering total of federal contract dollars as a way to offset declining commercial sales. An alert business executive sees a way to get into a new product line—by selling the concept to a federal agency that will foot all the development and nonrecurring costs.

As if the lure of huge government contracts alone were not enough to attract bevies of bidders, Uncle Sam calls attention to this prodigious spending at every opportunity. Libraries of books are released by federal agencies on how to sell to the government. More than 2000 trade associations flourish in Washington, and most are scurrying to find ways to help member firms land government contracts. There are 1800 trade journals in this country, virtually all of them at one time or another covering some aspect of industry–government dealings. An army of manufacturer representatives, consultants, and distributors tout their ability to help clients capture more of the federal dollar.

With such hoopla, one expects potential suppliers to fight like mad to grab their share of the huge contract funding. 'T'ain't necessarily so. Many federal agencies publicly express concern that the number of companies competing for government bids may be declining. Program offices have sometimes solicited up to 100 potential bidders and gotten back only half a dozen bids. Many procurements end up with only one or two bidders. Some don't attract a single response.

There are reasons for such economic illogic:

· Many small- and medium-sized companies fear the complexities of government business. Many simply don't know how to get into the marketplace. Some have heard horror stories of government procurement and run away from such a boogeyman. There may be a good excuse for shying away from some government bids, as we shall see, but shunning all potential government business—whether from ignorance, fear, uncertainty, or lack of experience—is playing the corporate ostrich and missing hundreds of thousands, even millions, of dollars in possible sales.

· Some business executives have gotten badly burned on a few federal bids and vow they will get out of the marketplace entirely. Selling to the government is never easy. We shall explore the innumerable pitfalls and booby traps that can snare even the most experienced vendor. To allow a few bad experiences to taint corporate marketing strategy is again turning away from vast potential business.

· Veteran contractors for the government also are getting more selective with regard to which procurements they will bid on and which they will pass up. Few firms have unlimited resources. As the expense of preparing and winning government bids increases, even the largest companies must choose which procurements they will bid on; vendors must know when there is a chance to win and when it is hopeless.

· The overwhelming mass of federal regulations, directives, and endless paperwork involved in federal bids scares away many qualified firms. Still, more than a million suppliers are coping with the maze of procurement rules and red tape. Even the smallest contractors—firms with fewer than ten employees—have learned how to deal with the System. Their experience should guide newcomers to the marketplace, as well as reacquaint long-time contractors with problems they tend to overlook.

Other economic contradictions are rife in government procurement. With the largest buying power in the world, the U.S. government should be able to command the least expensive price for the best products and services available. However, all too often the opposite occurs: Uncle Sam ends up paying a far higher price for products that are inferior or that simply don't work. Senator Howard Metzenbaum of Ohio said that Uncle Sam could get lower prices just by looking in the Yellow Pages instead of using normal bidding procedures.

Both government and industry share the blame. Federal agencies run up the cost of products and services (often paying three to five times more than comparable commercial customers) by unrealistic bid specifications and demands, by needless testing and paperwork, by stretching out procurement cycles for years, by inept management, by false starts and erratic program scheduling. Agencies are constantly changing their plans, modifying products, shifting quantities to be bought—all running up costs. Agency program offices sometimes write such poor bid specs that continual design changes must be made to make a product or service work. Again costs skyrocket.

Government-caused cost increases are great for contractors—if Uncle Sam picks up the tab. The more he bumbles, the more money contractors can make. Many vendors, as we shall see, count on government mistakes. They make rock-bottom initial price bids to win a contract, figuring all the government-sponsored changes later will pay off handsomely. This robs responsible vendors who submit realistically priced bids. It's all part of the game. Later chapters will explore the pros and cons of this system and what can be done.

Industry forces program cost hikes by overselling the potential capabilities of a product or service, by making overly optimistic estimates and promises, by taking on too much technical risk in a project that cannot be delivered, by trying to cut corners in using uncertain suppliers that don't work out, by hiding program troubles from the customer until it is too late for efficient remedies, by thwarting attempts for competitive bids that could bring lower program prices.

The hodgepodge of procurement rules and regulations, the elaborate bid process, the extensive government audits and regulations, and the elaborate disputes and claims process all make government business different from the commercial marketplace. Federal bureaucrats are far more apt to tell you how to run your business when you are working on their contracts—something business executives would rarely tolerate with commercial customers.

Many firms never learn how to tackle these obstacles successfully. They either are driven away from government business or flounder hopelessly. Some marketers to the government, however, thrive on the challenge. Gamesmanship reaches its highest art in selling to Uncle Sam. One veteran contractor confides: "I've never had a greater thrill than winning a government bid against every odd—and then beating down the buyocracy to deliver on the contract in spite of obstacles along the way."

WHY DO THEY DO IT?

For some firms the government is the only game in town; they have no other customer. Other companies turn to government marketing as commercial contracts slide. Some executives sincerely feel that they have a public duty to sell to the government despite some of the problems. Some do it purely for public relations. Some corporate officials want Uncle Sam to foot the bill for the start-up costs of developing a new product line that can be sold later in the commercial market. Other business officials see their arch-competitors enriching themselves off government contracts and decide to try their hands at the same game. Some firms have a special expertise or product, and Uncle Sam comes begging them to sell to the government.

A small company of sixty employees was funded by the Army to develop a military laser range finder to precisely measure the distance to a target. The firm was able to modify the same laser device into a highly accurate surveying instrument for many commercial markets. A manufacturer of warehouse racks convinced Navy supply depots to buy a flexible shelf bracket that would save installation costs. The Navy paid for the development, which the firm could use for commercial sales as well. Everyone was happy, the Navy saved warehouse costs and the vendor improved the product line.

Federal agencies can also become long-time customers—keeping equipment in place for decades while paying lease costs or the costs of continued training, documentation, spare parts, upgrading, and modifications, the service support expenditures over such extended periods. Companies that have amortized a product line decades ago can continue to sell it to the government at high profits—pure icing on the cake. Where commercial customers are frequently replacing equipment—often switching to a competitor—to keep up with corporate Joneses, government agencies may keep obsolete equipment long after it has disappeared from the commercial market. Some federal agencies still lease computers that IBM hasn't made in fifteen years, or lease comparable General Electric and RCA computers even though GE and RCA went out of the computer business years ago. The Air Force continues to fly many bombers with high-frequency radios containing vacuum tubes, even though commercial HF radios, the normal shortwave radios, haven't had vacuum tubes in twenty years.

There are other reasons for selling to Uncle Sam. First you don't have a customer credit risk. In fact, federal buyers may make periodic payments while the job is still going on. Occasionally, the government will even foot the start-up costs for a project. Frequently, agencies pay for materials being acquired before a project ever begins—or furnish all the material directly.

And whereas in the commercial jungle, vendors must grub and finagle to get sales leads, Uncle Sam readily obliges with leads for upcoming offers. Theoretically, federal bids are open to all qualified vendors, and there are supposed to be fairly well-defined rules to govern federal business. There are conditions attached to all these advantages, as we shall see later. But contractors find federal business attractive enough to sell to Uncle Sam. The smart ones have learned how to make it profitable as well. You can too.

2

PLUGGING IN
Getting Your Share Of
Procurement Dollars

• YOUR EARLY WARNING SYSTEM FOR UPCOMING BIDS: HOW
  AGENCIES DRAW UP THEIR REQUIREMENTS

• TRACKING AN EVOLVING BID THROUGH THE AGENCY

• SOME TOOLS FOR DIGGING UP BIDS—AND HOW TO USE THEM
  Commerce Business Daily
  Bidder mailing lists
  Prebid briefings
  Competitors

2. PLUGGING IN
Getting Your Share of Procurement Dollars

A small firm noticed government contracts going to rivals not any bigger and certainly not any better. The president decided to cash in on this marketing opportunity and took valuable time off to attend a conference on government procurement. He was told to apply to agencies that bought similar products and have the firm's name put on bidder mailing lists so the company would be notified of upcoming procurements. He also learned the importance of reading government publications, especially a daily report from the Commerce Department called *Commerce Business Daily*, which lists all notices of bids of more than $5000. Faithfully he filled out all forms and entered the *Commerce Business Daily* subscription. A year later the firm was still waiting to get its first government contract.

Government business does not fall in over the transom any more than commercial orders do. Vendors who sit back waiting to be notified of upcoming bids are behind before the competition starts. Their rivals have been talking to project officers, the agency superiors, the ultimate government users. They have been quietly touting their expertise while doing research on what the agency is thinking of buying.

Meanwhile, back at the home office, a proposal team may have already started to work with information gleaned by sales personnel calling on the agency. Subcontractors are being sounded out, and possible sources of supply are being scouted. Savvy vendors are already hard at work on proposals before the agency bid announcement ever hits the mails.

To succeed, your firm, no matter how small, must plug into this system. There is no great mystery to success. Thousands of contractors—an estimated 40,000 prime contractors for the Department of Defense alone—have learned how to work the system. Many of them have learned the hard way, by costly trial and error. You don't find the secrets for plugging into bids included in the countless government procurement guidebooks. But getting a jump on the bid process is the first commandment for success in selling to Uncle Sam.

Bids do not spring full-blown from the forehead of an agency Zeus, even if they often appear that way. Most bids go through long gestation periods and frequent false alarms and emergencies. Newcomers to selling to the government rarely see these behind-the-scene birth pains. Yet it is precisely during bid formation that agency contract offices are most susceptible in shaping the ultimate bid solicitation.

Follow a few typical bid gestations and see where openings exist to work with agencies in forming bid packages to your advantage. Also be aware of where to look for embryonic projects that will ultimately go out for bids.

THE BOTTOM-UP ROUTE: AGENCY USERS SET THEIR REQUIREMENTS

In the best of all procurement worlds, the agency users, whether front-line divisions in the Army or park rangers in the Interior Department, draw up their needs and agency buyers go out to secure required equipment and services. Ideally, the goods and services acquired match the users' stated needs. It rarely works that way, since both users and buyers within the agency have several tiers of bureaucracy, and each level plays its own games and works for its own self-interest.

The simplest bid for a small purchase, usually under $10,000, can be justified by the ultimate user with a minimum of review by higher levels. But even small items may get caught up in a full-scale, bottom-to-top agency review of the need. The agency may try to group all its scattered purchases of one type of equipment—test meters, auto oil filters, photocopy machines, burglar alarms, you name it—into one massive omnibus bid for all users.

The larger the equipment or service, the more levels of agency bureaucracy that will review the need. Requirements for even such straightforward products and services as fleet cars, architectural planning, and telephone networks, as well as missiles, computers, and field radios, go through exhaustive reviews.

Incredibly, many agencies have trouble drafting their precise requirements. At any one time various factions at the user level are bickering over conflicting needs. Users may come up with completely unrealistic desires. Often a hodgepodge of users will draft the requirements and the resulting verbal confusion or unintelligible compromise defies logic. The Federal Aviation Administration spent three years trying to draw up specific requirements for a new telephone switch to connect air traffic controllers across the country; they finally gave up and just ordered an older switch from the telephone company.

Every agency has its own term for the user requirement document. The Army calls it a ROC (Required Operational Capability). The Navy and Air Force call it an SOR (Standard Operating Requirement). NASA's word is PAD (Project Approval Document).

The name of the document may vary by agency, or even change within an agency as bureaucrats try to fine-tune the procurement process. Whatever the term used, at any one time thousands of these documents are struggling salmon-like up the bureaucratic river to spawn, far more than any agency could ever fund. So ROCs and SORs and PADs are dropped, shelved, combined, evaded, sent back for more study. A few are accepted—and not always because the need is the greatest. Often an agency moves forward on a project because this is the one with the best political chance for getting money. Sometimes the requirement strikes the fancy of agency superiors. Often the need is a "panic ploy" to meet political pressure and takes priority over all the ROCs and SORs and what-have-you in the works.

Officials at every level add their own pet desires to the wish list. By the time it is finished, the SOR or PAD or procurement request form may require a utopian product at infinite cost to meet every single need. Unfortunately, some efforts to scrub down dream lists are futile. No section chief who wants to be promoted to division chief knocks out the pet desire of the boss. No colonel who wants to make general tells the two-stars that their ideas are ridiculous.

> *Strategy:* Obviously, the requirements document resulting from intra-agency deliberations can tip off interested vendors on possible upcoming bids. The documents themselves are almost always kept confidential within the agency, but suppliers who have established good rapport with technical, purchasing, planning, and budget offices within the agency can often pick up inside dope on requirements being drawn up. Small firms cannot blanket agencies with marketing and technical scouts, but they can concentrate on a few agency offices that offer the most promising prospects. Close contact with as many parts of an agency as possible is essential.

THE TOP-DOWN ROUTE: AGENCY BUYERS KNOW BEST

Not all bids follow this textbook route. More often than not, the idea for a new product or service is born back at agency headquarters or in some lower contract office. A bureaucrat wants to build an empire and draws up a concept that goes searching for a need. The agency front office, closer to political power, often senses better than distant users what program can be sold to Congress, whether it is needed or not. Sometimes agency headquarters must spawn a new program because agency users fail miserably when asked to come up with a clearly stated requirement—for all the reasons we have seen.

A variation of the top–down route is for agency buyers to take a user's requirement and simply superimpose their own concepts on it, whether the evolved requirement meets the need or not. Common are the desk-bound admiral who claims to know what ships need better than the seagoing captain does; the whiz kid Ph.D. who knows that this new widget will meet the Air Force SOR; the doctor just put in charge of Veterans Administration hospital procurement who wants to throw out all the old clinical analytical equipment.

Users have virtually no control over the drawing up of their bid packages. Often the equipment they get bears little relationship to original specifications. Army front-line troops wanted a simple teleprinter that they could plug in to contact divisional command centers. They got a contraption that was so complex that it rarely worked, was three times the price that they had expected to pay, and did not have the features requested. To sidestep such problems, some users have squirreled away funds and tried to contract directly for needed equipment. The agency front office usually scotches this. It is an affront to headquarters authority and raises the specter of every user in the agency going out willy-nilly to buy all different kinds of equipment.

Clearly, the officials close to the seat of agency power hold most of the aces. Clever industry marketers will concentrate their presell on officials drafting the bid package—when unique features, detailed specs, and bid terms and conditions can be slipped in to give the firm a possible edge in any upcoming bid. To head off competitors, you must fight fire with fire: presell your position with agency buyers and contract officials partial to your approach.

Neophytes are often shocked at the thought of such close collusion between seller and buyer in the formulative bid stage, especially in the face of rigid standards of conduct and rules governing contractor-public employee contact. But such fraternization is not blatant. Properly handled, it is even lauded as a benefit in acquainting buying offices with the latest technical advances. Many agency program offices are so incompetent that they would be unable to get bids started without such contractor assistance.

This is how a vendor who offers a unique feature no competitor can provide often assures the firm's ultimate contract selection—by convincing the agency user or contract office to demand that feature as part of its requirement. Usually only large firms can play the "user strategy," for it requires far-flung marketing forces to presell agency users scattered across the country and perhaps the world. Smaller firms need not despair. By focusing on the agency buying office, which is usually concentrated in one location, smaller rivals often are able to use this technique too.

KING OF THE MOUNTAIN: EVERYBODY WANTS TO BE IN CHARGE

Yet another family fight may erupt before a bid package is started: which program office within the agency will handle the project? In any agency of any size at least several—perhaps half a dozen—offices are scrambling to control projects and prepare bids. Agency politics, personal loyalties, raw power plays, budgetary gamesmanship—all may carry as much weight as clear logic in deciding which office will control a new project.

Vendors, of course, want to be associated with the winning side, but trying to pick the winner of such an agency free-for-all is often difficult. Few firms have the resources to cover all possible candidate offices for a new project, so even large contractors must gamble with associations built up over the years. Naturally, the more ammunition (technical data, engineering projections, cost estimates, preliminary designs) a contractor supplies a contending bureaucrat in the power struggle, the stronger are their ties. A computer company virtually assured itself a Navy project office's business for years to come by tipping off officials that another part of the Navy was scheming to take over that office's mission.

SIGNED OFF: BACK TO THE DRAWING BOARD

Once agency brass approves a requirement—"signs off," in government parlance—the need is turned over to the procurement troops, who acquire the necessary equipment or service. That may not entail a competitive bid. Dozens of ploys and strategies are used by bureaucrats and industry marketers alike to meet the requirement without going out for bids. The program office simply awards a sole source contract to the firm it wants (see Chapter 4, "All's Fair in Love and Marketing").

When one looks at what a bid entails, it is a wonder any are ever issued. But they are, because of political pressure, a penchant to beat vendors down to the lowest possible price, or even a desire to abide by procurement rules that stress competition.

Bid solicitations are massive; they can be hundreds or even thousands of pages long. They cover every conceivable legal contingency, and then some. They tack on scores of legislated or Presidential requirements, from minority business subcontracting to pure-water standards to American Indian rights. The bid must specify as completely and concretely as possible the exact product or service desired. Rarely does an agency state its needs and leave it up to vendors to propose the best solution they can devise; that brings in too many varying approaches that agencies just can't judge. Also, buyers are far more comfortable writing specifications for an idealized product or service that they think will meet their need.

Drawing up such a detailed document, always with a multitude of opinions in the drafting process, drags on for what seems to waiting contractors an interminable period. This document must then go through a gamut of reviews, from branch to division to central office to headquarters, gathering changes and demands all the way. Even a routine bid solicitation document can wind its way up and down the bureaucratic channels several times before finally getting approved.

Strategy: Every level of review is a chance for knowledgeable vendors to slip in suggested conditions, specifications, or bid clauses favorable to them. At the very least, close contact with bureaucrats working on an embryonic bid will yield good intelligence—enough information for a firm to start its own preparations for an eventual proposal.

Federal regulations and agency rules, of course, put bid drafting strictly off limits to vendors, but nothing keeps company sales personnel making normal rounds of agency offices from watching for openings, playing on friendships, trading gossip. This is the stuff the commercial market is made of, and government selling is no different. Smaller firms may lack the far-flung marketing forces of their larger competitors, but they can judiciously play the same strategy in a limited way. The small firm may have to be content to work with the one agency lab it knows, with the local agency procurement people it can more readily reach. This firm may not be able to hire top-level agency people the way the big companies do but it can employ a lower level officer to work on agency contacts.

During these preliminary contacts, vendors try to find out:

- Whether the upcoming bid is for real or is merely the program office's desire to exercise industry "to see what we might get." Many vulnerable vendors spend thousands of dollars preparing extensive proposals in good faith, only to find out that project offices had no real intention of ever making a contract. Sometimes agency bid documents ask for the moon, when there is only enough budget to buy a fraction of what is spelled out in the bid package. Company marketing and technical people who have been at the elbows of officials as they prepare the bid package can get the inside dope on the real status of the proposed procurement.

- Details of infighting within an agency that could eventually submarine the bid. Other parts of an agency may have different ideas and concepts; they will maneuver behind the scenes to kill, change, or take over the project. Similarly, the program may face strong opposition at higher levels of authority within the agency. They may force a project to be canceled or sharply curtailed, even after it has come out for bid. At best, they can continually question the project or demand constant reviews, prolonging the bidding cycle.

- Other firms that might compete in an eventual bid. If nothing else, potential competitors are spotted doing the same detective work. Friendly project people can accidentally drop names of firms showing an interest in the bid. Being able to size up the competition right from the start can help a vendor plot bidding strategy before the solicitation ever comes out. Sometimes such early intelligence tells a firm it has little chance to win and to drop out before throwing away any more money. Or a small firm may decide that it has a better chance if, instead of bidding, it seeks to team up as a major subcontractor with a stronger contender.

DIVINING RODS FOR BIDS

Personal contact with agency staffers is still the best way to ferret out projected bids. However, firms must turn to other early warning sources for upcoming procurements.

Commerce Business Daily (CBD) is the traditional route the government uses to notify industry of upcoming bids. Legally, any procurement over $5000—whether by sole source or competitive bid—must be announced in *CBD*. A subscription to the five-times-a-week procurement chronicle can be obtained from the Superintendent of Documents; copies can be reviewed at local Commerce Department offices around the country.

Purchasing officers tout *CBD* as the way to learn of upcoming federal bids. But even newcomers can quickly size up its shortcomings. Bid notices are very cryptic, ambiguous, and sometimes misleading. Bids for one type of equipment can end up listed in the wrong category—a classic *CBD* misplacement listed bids for steel beams under wearing apparel. *CBD* readers must squint through most of its twenty to thirty pages of agate type to avoid missing any bids of interest to them.

CBD bid alerts often give only a few days' or weeks' notice before the bid closing deadline—far too little time for a firm learning of the bid for the first time to respond. *CBD* is supposed to give the address and phone number of a contracting office where the bid solicitation can be obtained. Frequently, the addresses are too general, simply listing "Naval Sea Systems Command, Washington, DC 20362." This is too vague for the vendor, let alone the post office carrying the vendor's letter of interest, to know where to send the letter. The safest bet is to pick up the bid solicitation in person if *CBD* lists a sufficient address. Many letters requesting bid packages listed in *CBD* never find their way through the bureaucratic maze to the right office. Some agencies simply don't answer. Often, mailed bid solicitations are so delayed that a firm has no chance to respond.

Bidder mailing lists kept by agencies are not much better.

Agencies make a big deal of putting a firm on various mailing lists under appropriate product categories so the firm will be solicited on upcoming bids. But project offices may not use the agency mailing list at all, or they may sample only part of the list. Many times a contractor is put on the wrong list and gets no bids in the right area of capabilities. Mailing and address errors are common. The Navy once mailed a nuclear reactor bid invitation to a General Electric appliance dealer in New Jersey instead of to the firm's nuclear reactor division.

Agencies and program offices are getting better about giving longer advance notice on some projected bids. Many contracting offices put an alerting notice in *CBD* months before bids will be solicited. Interested firms can specifically ask to receive the bid solicitation when issued. Other program offices hold prebid conferences and briefings that are open to any interested firm. Attending companies can ask to receive the bid document and get advance information on the project early enough to do them some good.

> *Caution:* Many firms send staffers halfway across the country for a prebid briefing, and then wait and wait for the expected bid solicitation. It may never come out. Or it may be so radically changed from the briefing conference description that a firm has no chance to bid. Patience is a necessary attribute in dealing with Uncle Sam.

Agencies, trade associations, and publications stage a welter of symposiums and seminars to outline future programs and projects. Typical briefings: "A Ten-Year Forecast of Federal Aviation Administration Programs" or "New Automation Projects at the U.S. Postal Service." Such show-and-tell sessions may give a clue to the agency's wish list at that moment but are uncertain indicators of possible upcoming bids. Agency plans and strategies change so rapidly, budgets fluctuate so widely that a host of projects unveiled at such seminars never get off the drawing boards.

Competitors can be a surprising source of information on upcoming bids. There is enough cross-hiring of people among companies that everyone soon knows most of the programs that all companies are following. Many competitors decide to join together on large bids, so companies are sounding each other out on many projects. Since government bids must be made public, the usual secrecy surrounding the commercial market is relaxed. Industry conventions, cocktail lounges, telephoning friends at rival companies all provide tips on upcoming procurements.

No matter what prospecting tools vendors use, they must do some spadework if they want to sell to Uncle Sam. The earlier a firm can spot and work to influence an evolving bid, the greater are its chances for success. Winston Churchill declared at the outset of World War II that intelligence "is the sinews of victory." Never was this more true than in the race for government business.

3

FACT AND FICTION
You've Got to Know the Ground Rules before You Even Start

MYTH 1: There Is One Government Market

MYTH 2: All Qualified Bidders Are Equal, with Inalienable Rights to Sell to the Government

MYTH 3: Most Government Business Is by Advertised Competitive Bid

MYTH 4: You Can Make a Killing in Federal Markets

MYTH 5: Bureaucrats and Contractors Want to Save Taxpayers' Money

3. FACT AND FICTION
You've Got to Know the Ground
Rules before You Even Start

Most newcomers, and a surprising number of old-timers, are misled by a collection of government procurement myths. This mythology, like the legends of history and religion, contains rituals, euphemisms, and a few outright deceptions that cover up the deeper animosities, conflicting motives, and psychological underpinnings of buyer and seller.

These myths are like the fine phrases in stockholder reports, necessary window dressing for public consumption. As long as buyers and contractors do not mistake the oft-repeated legends for the real world, all goes well. Disaster inevitably follows when one or both sides come to believe the marketing fables they have created.

To help you enter government selling with your eyes open, here are a few of the most common myths.

MYTH 1: THERE IS ONE GOVERNMENT MARKET

Everyone talks about *the* government market. Companies try to sell the government market. Economists try to predict its future course and federal officials themselves talk of budgets, rules, and problems as if a homogeneous, unified market existed.

The fact is that there are hundreds, probably thousands, of different government markets. Each agency, almost every program office within an agency, is a separate market. Each has its own character, direction, problems. Each is distinct from any other part of the vast federal establishment.

Smart government vendors quickly learn that strategies that work for one program office won't necessarily work for another. A veteran contractor of electric generators finds one Army depot buying strictly on the basis of lowest price; an Air Force base supply office stresses reliability; the Veterans Administration wants quick delivery; a regional Postal Service office doesn't want to bother with bids at all and just buys generators sole-source from hand-picked suppliers. On other procurements the very same buying offices may change tactics drastically, depending on their budgets, the contracting officials running the bid, or new political pressures on the agency.

Such changeable customers can unnerve the best corporate executive. It's far more comfortable for top management to plan around a monolithic government market, even if it doesn't exist. Trying to track hundreds of shifting federal markets is no easy task.

The salesperson on the firing line, even the marketing director, may be unable to convince the front office how inconsistent federal buyers can be. A Washington office manager moans, "We won a $6 million Department of Energy contract making our big pitch on a novel technical approach for a new solar furnace. Now my boss can't understand why we lost another bid at the same agency to a competitor who simply low-balled the price, which is what the contracting officer apparently wanted this time."

Procurement rules also vary widely from agency to agency. True, two immense compilations of regulations—the Federal Procurement Regulations (FPR) for civilian agencies and the Defense Acquisition Regulation System (DARS)* for military services—are supposed to govern all transactions. The sheer mass of these main procurement Bibles (the DARS alone runs 3000 pages in three volumes) can frighten off all but the hardiest vendors. But even if business executives could fathom the bulk of FPR and DARS, they would still find individual buying offices playing by yet a different set of rules. Most of the 450 federal agencies and bureaus have their own procurement rules. These directives must conform to the central FPR and DARS—but each adds its own wrinkles and interpretations.

Be aware that procurement rules vary, but don't panic. This diversity can be an asset to vendors. If a firm has done its selling job at the agency project office, if it has good rapport with the contracting officer, then company officials should have some idea how the game is played. It is the individual contract officer you must sell, not that distant bureaucrat who drew up some procurement edict. A small medical instrument firm president admitted he could never divine all the procurement regs. "But my firm had great relations

---

* Formerly called Armed Services Procurement Regulations (ASPR). At this writing the Office of Management and Budget is engaged in a massive effort to combine the civilian FPR and military DARS into a single Federal Acquisition Regulation (FAR).

with a National Institutes of Health lab. Regardless of the number of directives curbing sole-source purchases, the lab procurement people would find a way to sole-source our instruments."

Many small firms are needlessly paralyzed by fear of the huge government market. In reality, the government market is hundreds upon hundreds of small marketplaces. A vast number of these minimarkets are easily managed by small contractors who know how. Smaller vendors are often intimidated by agency contracting officers who clothe themselves in all the power of the federal establishment. Small contracting firms should remember that an individual agency project office is not some formidable monolith. The firm is dealing with only one contracting officer, not all 3 million federal employees.

MYTH 2: ALL QUALIFIED BIDDERS ARE EQUAL WITH INALIENABLE RIGHTS TO SELL TO THE GOVERNMENT

Logically, not all vendors are equal. A ten-person machine tool shop is not equal to the nation's corporate giants in bidding on any government order. Yet there persists a mythical Bill of Procurement Rights that holds that every qualified firm, no matter how much the underdog, has equal time at bat on a government bid. Uncle Sam spends millions of dollars on pamphlet propaganda and traveling seminars trying to convince newcomers to the marketplace that they have just such equal treatment. Without such assurance, bureaucrats fear that new firms might not be attracted into government bidding to keep competition strong.

However, the real inequity is not between large and small firms or even between entrenched contractors and newcomers. (Many times small firms beat larger rivals, and old-time contractors find themselves brushed aside like a stepchild in a federal bid.) The real procurement world has a hierarchy of contractors. Once a firm recognizes what caste it occupies with regard to any bid, company officials can better assess the risks, position, and probable fate of the sale. Success is knowing your real place—and acting on that knowledge. The three broad castes of contractors follow.

Privileged. A government agency cannot live without these contractors. They may be the only supplier of a critical product or service. They may have dealt with an agency so long that the relationship has nearly fused company and agency goals, staff, and planning. Privilege may come from political power. A firm is so large in one state that Congressional representatives will use extraordinary persuasion to assist it in dealings with the federal agencies. A firm may be so large across the country that both the White House and Congress feel "What's good for Company X is good for the country."

Primes. Most contractors fall in the vast middle class of procurement. They lack the clout of the privileged elite, but are not low firm on the buying totem pole either. Agency project officials will consider a prime's sales pitch but are under no pressure to give in. A prime wins by wits and skill, not by its standing in the hierarchy. However, if forced into a shootout against a privileged firm, the prime loses every time.

Prols. At rock bottom of the procurement pecking order are the prols—the dispensable contractors whose fate concerns neither their industry brethren nor anyone in government. They live in Orwell's *1984*, performing the bulk of menial, routine work of keeping the government running, without praise, reward, or acknowledgment. Should prols stumble at any contracting task, they can quickly be swept aside. Their place is readily filled by other willing prols, tackling the same thankless task for the same menial payment, just to survive.

The strategy of vendors is obvious: become privileged as much as possible, avoid becoming a prol, and play the role of prime realistically.

Fortunately, even the smallest supplier can become privileged in some situations. One firm of forty employees supplying an essential component to a shipboard fire control system not only got all the funding it needed for costly contract overruns; it also sold nonvoting preferred stock to the Navy to raise equity funds. The small vendor whose proprietary part is essential to a key project is as privileged as the largest Department of Defense contractor.

Conversely, the biggest vendor can find itself playing the role of prol on some contracts, when work can be rejected or canceled at no cost to the government. Top managements of privileged firms too often grow lax, only to be jolted by a setback in a new marketplace where they lack standing.

Knowing your place in the procurement register is knowing

what treatment to expect from contract offices on any given bid or contract. A firm can plan a realistic strategy and not be duped into a no-win situation.

Rarely is a contractor completely locked into one caste. A company is privileged, prime, and perhaps even prol simultaneously. Such procurement schizophrenia can drive management mad. Few executives can concurrently dominate as privileged on one contract and grovel as prols on another. Split roles create havoc when a firm can sock it to an agency for excess costs on one pact but must eat them all on another. If there is any saving grace, it is simply that roles shift so rapidly that even the lowliest contractors on one project can improve their lot on the next bid.

It's even possible to break contracting caste barriers on the same project. A prol or a prime struggles for years on one contract, then suddenly finds itself the only remaining supplier. Or buyers, for any of a hundred different emergencies, must get immediate delivery. Now the contractor is elevated to privileged status, perhaps by accident. The rule is: Castes do change as situations change. You can move up the procurement ladder.

MYTH 3: MOST GOVERNMENT BUSINESS IS BY ADVERTISED COMPETITIVE BID

At this writing, the federal law mandates that all procurement must be by straight, advertised bids; low price automatically wins. Therefore, it comes as a shock to many newcomers to learn that only 16 percent of all federal procurement dollars go out for advertised competitive bids. The overwhelming bulk of federal buying is done under fifteen specified "exemptions" to the law—by sole-source contracts directed to one firm or through competitive negotiations with several firms.

Many neophytes jump into the federal marketplace in the mistaken notion that buying is open to all qualified vendors through straight competitive bids. "All I must do to win is underbid everyone else."

Not so. Most federal business—more than 80 percent of all procurement dollars—comes through the Request for Proposal (RFP) exemption. Under RFP bids, buyers are free to award contracts to the firm they feel has the most qualified proposal regardless of price. In some cases, the high-price RFP bidder wins the award.

RFPs come in every size, shape, and description. Some are one page long. Others run to thousands of pages, replete with legal jargon and bureaucratic gobbledegook. Some are highly detailed; others are vague and ambiguous. Some tell bidders exactly what the program office wants them to build; others leave it to bidders to propose their own ideas.

All this tends to make government buying far more complex and incredibly more confusing than simple advertised competitive bids. In spite of the problems, however, hundreds of companies master the maze and a surprising number come through winners. Even though only 16 percent of federal dollars is spent through open, low-price-takes-all bids, this 16 percent amounts to millions of dollars' worth of business. And when newcomers learn to navigate the RFP maze (the subject of most of this book), they will find that the total procurement pot contains billions of dollars, more than enough for their firms and hundreds like theirs.

MYTH 4: YOU CAN MAKE A KILLING IN FEDERAL MARKETS

Undoubtedly, a few privileged contractors have grown fat at the public trough. The illusion of immense windfalls in federal business is also fueled by political attacks on large contractors charged with bilking the government. The facts are: Government business is far less profitable, on the average, than commercial markets for similar products and services. A wealth of studies, by government and industry alike, show that companies may earn half as much profit selling identically the same product to Uncle Sam as to a commercial customer. There are reasons: intense competition, the mass of paperwork, extra demands, prolonged bidding cycles, omnipresent Monday-morning quarterbacks in government, shifting demands, and changing designs.

The only profit killing in federal procurement may come from contract officers squeezing contractors to get the lowest possible price, in many cases forcing a firm to kill what little profit it may be making. Neophytes expecting to get rich quick in federal markets are in for a shock.

To make any profit at all, contractors must know what angles to play in their proposals. They must know their rights and bargain hard in negotiations to get a fair deal. They must know how to live with a myriad of government contracting, auditing, and inspecting officials. They must know where Uncle Sam will allow them to recoup losses and where he won't. Then vendors can make money in federal procurement, even if it is not a killing.

Uncle Sam does offer some financial benefits not usually found elsewhere. Instead of having to wait until a job is completed to get paid, most federal contractors get periodic payments, called progress payments, while the work is being done. This helps cash flow, reduces the need to borrow working capital, and cuts some financial risks. Agencies may furnish tooling, machinery, raw materials, component subsystems, even part of the work force. These financial plusses often offset the lower profits generally earned in government work.

MYTH 5: BUREAUCRATS AND CONTRACTORS WANT TO SAVE TAXPAYERS' MONEY

The favorite party line of everyone dealing with public funds is a passionate stewardship of the tax dollar. Industry and government meetings ring with oratory on spending tax money wisely. Actually, nothing is further from the truth. The chief interest of most bureaucrats is enlarging their own position, which often entails prodigious spending. The goal of most vendors is to increase contract funding.

Both motivations are far too crass to be politically tolerable, so they are couched in typical doublethink. Every massive program expansion, every staggering contract increase is hailed as "saving the taxpayers' money." This much higher spending will "bring greater system performance" . . . or "cut future maintenance and repair costs" . . . or "replace old equipment that is costly to operate." Sometimes this is true, sometimes not.

A major Army communication system jumped 250 percent in cost—from $50 million to $125 million. Officials patted themselves on the back because the extra money would be used to design a simpler system that supposedly would cost less to deploy. But the spiraling development costs more than offset any alleged savings. The Navy's Trident submarine-launched long-range missile shot up $8 billion over original cost estimates. Navy officials justified the added price because taxpayers would get a far superior nuclear missile for the money. When tests proved that the Trident, instead of showing greater target accuracy, was getting poorer accuracy, Navy apologists praised the fact that the service was not rushing into production, but was thoroughly testing the prototype—at greater expense, of course.

This lack of accountability to anyone except other government officials is probably the weakest part of the procurement system and the part that drives many conscientious firms out of the federal market. This is unfortunate because the basic system will change only when enough concerned citizens understand enough of the system to demand change. Many times, contract irregularities occur because not enough disgruntled competitors have watched what is going on. Many times, agencies and vendors team up to the detriment of the taxpayers, and no one is involved enough to blow the whistle. Nearly every major contracting scandal brought to public attention has been ferreted out by a concerned competitor. Sure, there is a big sour-grapes component in all this; nevertheless, good is done, and the good is that after every Congressional investigation, after every major protest, things do get better. If it gives you any comfort, many conscientious people within each agency are as concerned about procurement problems as you are. These secret allies will make themselves known when your sales personnel start working the field. Since bucking the system is a good way to ruin a promotion or get transferred to Civil Service Siberia, these agency employees themselves cannot bring problems to the attention of their superiors or GAO, but they are delighted to have you protest for them.

Ideally, the procurement process should strive to get the best product at the lowest price for the government, but since the system is far from perfect—and since this book deals with the real world of procurement—we will dispense with the idea of saving the money of John and Jane Taxpayer. When the public can get changes made at the real root of the system, then untold savings of public funds will automatically follow.

4

ALL'S FAIR IN LOVE AND MARKETING
The Art of Getting a Contract
before a Bid Even Goes Out

- SOLE-SOURCE PURCHASES: HOW TO GET YOUR SHARE
  (AND HOW TO STOP YOUR COMPETITOR'S SOLE SOURCE)

- NONCOMPETITIVE BIDS: HOW TO LOCK IN A PROCUREMENT
  FOR YOUR COMPANY

- GRABBING A CONTRACT AWAY FROM AN INCUMBENT VENDOR

- EVEN THE SMALL FIRM CAN GET IN ON THE SOLE-SOURCE GAME

4. ALL'S FAIR IN LOVE AND MARKETING
The Art of Getting a Contract before
a Bid Even Goes Out

The business executive who waits for bid packages to erupt from government buying offices is missing one of the best ways to land a contract—getting it signed before a bid even comes out.

Experienced contractors work hard to convince buying offices that no bid is necessary; a sole-source award can meet agency needs with far less fuss and trouble. Every year some $40 billion in government business is done this way—it never goes out for bid at all.

Agencies like sole-source awards because they are quick, they go to contractors that can be trusted, they don't end up in messy protests, and they avoid the hassle of drawing up complicated bid packages. There is little danger of ending up with a low-price bidder who cannot deliver on the job.

Vendors love sole sources—if they get them. Companies are also spared the high costs of stretched-out bidding cycles, protests, unfavorable terms. Of course, your competitor's sole source is a travesty of the procurement process, a violation of all federal procurement regulations. The only good sole source is your own.

THE SOLE-SOURCE GAME: YOU CAN'T
TELL THE PLAYERS WITHOUT A SCORECARD

To play the sole-source game, you have to understand the team you are playing against—the bureaucrats who run all parts of a project. Federal government procurement, after all, is *people*—contract officers, technical staffs, agency executives, auditors, inspectors, contract administrators—the buyocrats.

They come in every shape and size and from a myriad of backgrounds, carry with them all the troubles and anxieties of the day, make mistakes, and struggle to achieve satisfaction. They react to the same Parkinson's Law. They follow the same Peter Principle inherent in any organization.

A common fear pervades all bureaucracy: the black mark on a personnel record. That alone can disturb an otherwise normal progression up the government career ladder. The government has none of the conventional benchmark goals of the commercial marketplace—no sales quotas, no profit targets, no productivity ratings. The buyocrat's real stimulus is a negative factor: avoiding a bad proficiency report. And nothing creates a career black mark like a problem contract. No wonder that project offices are leary of bids that could be won by inexperienced prols or unknown firms; they could jeopardize a long career record. A sole source given to a trusted privileged or prime firm is the buyocrat's security blanket.

Smart contractors cater to the bureaucrat's self-interest to promote sole-source awards. A renowned commercial airline got a $20 million contract to ferry service people across the Atlantic by suggesting that it had a known record and was less risky than charter airline rivals. An Air Force missile test range gave a Fortune 500 firm a sole-source contract to develop a special telemetry radio that the firm had never built before—despite pleas from a small company that actually had in stock the radio the Air Force said it wanted.

Small firms can play on buyocrats' instinct for survival for smaller sole-source awards. Agency lab technicians can be convinced to order test instruments and supplies from small, quality manufacturers. A program office in trouble with a large contractor may rush a sole-source award to a much smaller firm that can salvage the project.

Most sole sources require special justification by the agency contracting office. The most adroit contracts are so disguised that higher authorities rarely question them, but any contract officer worthy of the name can conjure up enough convincing reasons for a sole source that the findings will be accepted by superiors. In the Pentagon the sole-source justification is called "Determination and Finding," or D&F. Just to be different, civilian agencies reverse it: "Finding and Determination," or F&D.

Sample justifications: the agency has immediate need for the product or service and cannot wait for a long competitive bid; the vendor getting the sole-source award allegedly is the only firm able to supply the equipment; the agency has existing high investment in test equipment, software, or similar equipment that will be compatible only with the sole-source gear; the agency is simply buying more of the same products or services it has already ordered in the past. Defense agencies hide behind the unchallengeable blanket of "national security." More blatant D&Fs are filed by buyers who claim they have "surveyed the market" and found the sole-source equipment best suited to their needs.

SOLE-SOURCE SORTIES: HOW TO GET YOUR SHARE

Here are some of the best ways to snag sole-source awards.

The Unsolicited Proposal. A vendor has a unique idea for a product, makes the pitch to the agency, and gets a sole-source award to try it out. Such unsolicited proposals are a valid way of doing business with Uncle Sam. Indeed, agencies get some of their most successful projects from concepts volunteered by vendors. Imaginative firms frequently come up with ideas of their own that agencies would never conceive of.

However, buyocrats and vendors alike can use unsolicited proposals to circumvent all the competitive bidding regulations. Program offices can then keep extending the contract year after year, thwarting further competition. One large computer firm sold an initial $97,000 sole-source unsolicited proposal—and parlayed that into $4 million in additional sole-source funding over the next three years.

Unsolicited proposals can be made to one agency for funding to help put a firm in a good position for a competitive bid at another agency. That way, Uncle Sam actually helps pay for much of the shrewd firm's preproposal spadework for an upcoming bid. The Army wanted to develop a new battlefield computer to run complex new software; one smart vendor got an entirely different agency, the Naval Research Lab, to accept an unsolicited proposal to pay for adapting the software to its computer.

An unsolicited proposal to modify an existing contract is the quickest way to head off any future competitive bids. An incumbent supplier suggests ways that the present equipment can be "easily" modified for upgraded capability, thus hoping to prevent any future bid for replacement gear. A firm may suggest that its equipment be adapted to meet an entirely different need of the same agency or another federal program office, thus fending off any future competitive bid. The pitch of any such unsolicited proposal is always how easily the equipment can be modified; if the buyer bites, the resulting adaptation may turn out to be almost an entirely new product.

No matter. Once an agency accepts the unsolicited proposal, it is hooked and often willingly goes along with such ruses—they really wanted a sole-source contract in the first place.

Caution: Be sure you have privileged or prime status. Prols or vendors that aren't locked in with the customer may find buyers stealing the best ideas of their unsolicited proposals as the basis for competitive bids—or, horrors, for sole-source awards to rival contractors.

Counterploy: Contractors can rarely learn of competitors' unsolicited proposals in time to try to block them, but companies must work diligently to block rivals from parlaying unsolicited proposals into expanded sole-source procurements that preempt future business. Protest to higher agency superiors; sometimes they aren't aware of the covert sole source secreted by lower agency program offices. Counter with your own unsolicited proposal to try to force an open competitive shoot-out of proposals. Challenge any extension of a rival's unsolicited proposal; question the adequacy of the program office's sole-source justification.

Unsolicited proposals have a peak harvest time: right before the end of the government's fiscal year. Agencies and program offices that haven't used up all their budgeted funds by then may stand to lose the money allocation, so buyocrats often jump at even unlikely unsolicited proposals at this time, just to get the funds committed.

Companies should make an adequate-to-excellent profit on contracts resulting from unsolicited proposals, since there is no competition beating down prices. Small firms should be careful not to price unsolicited offers so high that big companies would be interested in the business. One small business kept pricing unsolicited proposals higher and higher until an offer of $75,000 attracted larger competitors, which forced the agency to go out for competitive bids on the concept. On the other end of the scale, vendors can price unsolicited proposals so low that program offices figure it isn't worth the paperwork and administrative costs to handle such a small contract. One small energy research firm tried to peddle a $15,000 proposal to the Commerce Department, but no project manager wanted to bother with administering such a small contract. The firm went to another office down the hall, pumped up the concept to $50,000, and got a contract.

Riding Piggyback. This can be done on orders off another contract, either with the same agency or with a different agency. Rich agencies are constantly upgrading to bigger and better gear. Installed older leased equipment can be switched to less affluent agencies, which pick up the unexpired lease sole-source. This ploy often is touted as helping the government "reutilize surplus equipment." Of course, rental equipment can usually be sent back to the lessor, but contract offices that really want to sole-source the gear overlook this and claim great benefits by using so-called surplus equipment from other agencies. A clever firm can almost set up a perpetual-motion marketing chain throughout the government—upgrading sole-source at one agency, then shifting the replaced equipment sole-source to other agencies—thus preventing competitive bids there as well.

*Sole-Source Purchases Disguised as Competition Through Orders From General Services Administration Federal Supply Schedule (FSS) Contracts.** Vendors can negotiate annual master FSS contracts with GSA for various product lines; GSA has more than 8500 schedule contracts totaling $1.6 billion, covering more than 4 million products and services. Federal buyers can then order directly from a firm's GSA schedule contract—within limits—without having to conduct a competitive bid. The biggest limit is the maximum order level on any purchase, which varies by type of product or service. An agency is also not supposed to avoid competitive bids by breaking up a big procurement into a series of smaller purchases from the GSA schedule contract to stay under the maximum order limitation.

Buying offices are fond of calling the GSA schedule contracts "multiple competitive awards," since GSA does negotiate with a plethora of companies. In practice, most GSA schedule contracts are awarded at nearly the commercial list prices for each company, with an occasional small extra discount thrown in by various vendors. Thus, federal buyers ordering off a firm's GSA schedule contract are paying nearly the regular list price. No matter how euphemistically GSA schedules are called "multiple awards," a buyer is still making a sole-source purchase by dealing with only one specified vendor.

* See Chapter 5, "A Baedecker on Bids."

Getting the Product Specified as Standard for Future Government Bids. This can be done in many ways. An adroit vendor will try to get a superagency or cabinet department to make its product a standard for all procurement offices in the agencies or among several agencies. Your pitch should be how a single, standard product will simplify logistics,. cut maintenance and training costs, and make future ordering easier—all saving gobs of taxpayer money. Of course, once a product is locked in as standard, the contractor may be able to jack up the price sharply without facing competition.

Component and part makers can obtain the same result by getting agencies to specify their product as standard or preferred supply for prime contractors, or by having a brand-name part specified on engineering drawings supplied to prime contracts. One savvy parts manufacturer withdrew a $73,000 claim against an agency in return for having his part specified on engineering drawings for all future procurements, more than making up for the lost claim.

Even Prols Can Play the Sole-Source Game. They must convince buyers to make part of a bid or the entire procurement a small business set-aside.* This restricts bidding to firms qualified as small business concerns. Often only a single small company makes the product, so the set-aside becomes a sole-source award.

> *Counterploy:* Obviously, if a competitor is getting a sole-source award, you must fight it vigorously to prevent your firm's being locked out of potential business. The most effective time to stop sole-sourcing is before an award is made. After a contract is signed, it is nearly impossible to turn it around. Vendors must have good intelligence within an agency to discover when such an award is pending. Since buying offices usually must draw up formal justification for sole source, documents are floating around an agency—if a friendly subordinate can alert you. By law, agencies must put a notice in *Commerce Business Daily* whenever they select any firm to negotiate a sole-source contract for more than $5000. Gossip with friends in industry may tip you off when one of your regular rivals is in line for a sole-source contract. When you fight, it is futile to protest to the contracting office, no matter how much lower your price is or how much better your product is. The buyer has already

* See Chapter 18, "Small Business: It's a Small, Small Whirl."

decided and is more interested in avoiding problems of a competitive bid, not in getting a better product or a lower price. Try to bring pressure from higher authorities. (See Chapter 12, " 'I've Been Robbed!': The Art of Protesting.")

MORE SOLE SOURCES: PLAYING TO THE AUDIENCE

A variation of the sole-source game is proposing to build a design or plan drawn up by the agency itself. Nothing appeals more to the bureaucrats than a scheme that they have conceived, although they may be cool or even antagonistic to industry-conceived ideas. But all too often the agency cannot build the product; it must depend on a contractor to turn drawings and plans into hardware, even for prototypes or engineering models. For this game the agency design does not even have to work; in fact, a contractor may lose out completely by trying to suggest major changes to make the concept operable.

A firm that finds such a glint in a buyocrat's eye can offer to make the dream a reality. Often this is done simply through an unsolicited proposal—parroting back the scheme the agency conjured up in the first place. This eliminates the annoying problem of competitive bids and the risk of an unknown firm that might louse up the pet concept. Sometimes the agency acts as its own prime contractor but awards the major portion of work sole-source to a favored firm. Often an entrenched company has an open-ended support contract with an agency, and millions of dollars' worth of new work is quietly started sole-source as "just another duty" under the umbrella support contract. One communications firm kept enlarging its engineering service support contract at the Defense Communications Agency until it had $14 million of sole-source work annually in a dozen different areas.

Another sole-source variation is rescue, or "I can save your neck if you buy my proposal."

All procurement edicts for competitive bids are bent or sidestepped when the agency is under fire because a key program is faltering. If the troubled project cannot be salvaged, buyers must take immediate action to save their necks. They often jump at an alternative proposal. At the very least, it creates a diversion from their immediate crisis.

The Post Office ran into serious problems trying to put together a completely automated letter-sorting system. A major systems integrator got more than $8 million in sole-source business by volunteering to make the complicated mail-handling system work. Never mind that the sole-source rescuer bombed out as well; the firm collected handsome profits in the meantime.

Often a firm that suspects an agency is facing a troubled project can get a foot in the door early in the game. The company sells a limited sole-source study contract that attracts no attention or protest. The alternative approach is then pursued on government funds, not on the company's own money. When the original troubled program develops death rattles, the alternative concept is rushed out for a crash effort. Naturally, a sole-source award is made because of the urgent need, and the study contractor is "the only firm with the necessary knowledge and background" to proceed.

NONCOMPETITIVE BIDS: HOW TO LOCK IN
A PROCUREMENT FOR YOUR COMPANY

Even if buyers are afraid to make a sole-source award, they can oblige a favored firm by rigging the bid in its favor. Imaginative program officials can devise an almost infinite number of ways to slant bids.

Instant Bids—Now You See It, Now You Don't. The most common abuse is putting a short deadline on a proposal. Agencies have demanded that highly complex proposals for large communication complexes be submitted in one or two weeks. The Social Security Administration wanted computer firms to submit bids only three days after the RFPs were released for some of the largest systems made. The National Institute of Mental Health wanted a computer so fast that it telephoned vendors with proposal deadlines of only a matter of hours. In these cases a favored firm has probably been preparing its proposal months before the instant bid came out; the quick deadline only prevents most rivals from bidding.

Buyocrats have no shortage of reasons to justify such instant bids: immediate urgent need, pending loss of budgeted funds, imminent expiration of special discounts by the favored vendor. The more brazen ones simply don't bother justifying such short-fuse bids; they know agency superiors won't challenge bid deadlines of only a few days.

Of course, the very same contract office imposing immediate

bid deadlines took months, even a year or more, to lay out the project in the first place. Much of the professed urgency is the fault of foot-dragging and inertia in getting the bid solicitation ready and approved. But higher government authorities rarely see the dichotomy of the contract office dawdling on bid preparation while demanding instant response from vendors once bids are finally invited.

Suppliers also wonder about many quickie bid deadlines when agencies then take weeks or even months before awarding a contract. And why are instant bid deadlines set when delivery of equipment or services is not needed for months?

Special Features Required: Only the Favored Firm Has Them. This is strictly a sole source disguised as a competitive bid. The contract office knows full well that only the desired firm can supply the equipment or service mandated. If challenged, agencies will claim that these features are essential for a variety of reasons, and few in government are willing to question contracting office judgment. Occasionally a key member of Congress or a high agency official who is antagonistic to the contracting office will throw out a bid that brazenly dictates a single product. The strategy of the favored firm is to help buyocrats couch the RFP in terms just broad enough to avoid a legal challenge but narrow enough to wire in the desired product or service.

A variation is to write the bid package so that it is open to true competition on almost all equipment except for one critical piece. Only one company makes the essential item, so no matter how competitive the rest of the bid is, the favored vendor has it locked in.

Brand Name or Equal Bids: Dictating the Desired Product by Name. This greatly simplifies bid writing, since buyers merely identify the product by model number. Theoretically, the bid is open to competition because another vendor can propose its product if the product is equal to the specified brand-name item. Unfortunately, the burden of proof is often on the rival firm, which must prove its product is "equal" to the mandated brand-name item. Good buyocrats can find some deviation to justify rejection of almost identical products because they "are not equal." The General Accounting Office and the courts have been leary of questioning buying office judgments. Both arbiters claim that they lack the technical expertise to overturn such decisions.

Strategy: If a program office is a known low-price grabber, a rival firm may beat out even a "brand-name-or-equal" product by really bombing a low price. If a contract office is merely using "brand name or equal" because it is too lazy to draw up a more detailed bid specification, then rival firms have a chance to unseat the specified brand-name product through price, special terms, higher performance.

Specify Actual Hardware Bid Samples with Special Features. If a rival firm doesn't have an exact product in its catalog, it may be forced to risk large sums trying to adapt its product in a short time to supply a bid sample. Just to be sure, the agency sets an impossibly short deadline. The State Department gave firms a deadline of two days, which only the favored vendor could meet, to submit bid samples for a complex burglar alarm. In the unlikely event that an unwanted rival does meet such an instant deadline, agency evaluators run highly partial inspection tests. Unless such tests are blatantly biased (and good buyocrats can cover their tracks well enough in testing), few authorities in government will second-guess the agency evaluation.

Making It Too Rough for Rival Firms to Bid. This clears the way for a favored vendor. The Chinese torture tactics in bidding are almost endless. Buyers can ask scores of highly technical questions, giving contenders very little time to respond. If this doesn't discourage unwanted bidders, the contracting office then rejects their answers as nonresponsive or inadequate. Bid packages can be drawn up to overpower undesired contenders; one bid included 300 feet of microfilm drawings and gave the vendor only three weeks to review all of it and prepare the bid. Normal bids are massive volumes anyway—it doesn't take many more documents to chase off most firms and leave the way clear for the desired contractor. At the other extreme, program offices can hoard necessary technical data to prevent unwanted contenders from bidding. Critical engineering drawings may be available for inspection only at the program office. Sample items to be reproduced may not be made available. A common ploy to chase off novice firms is simply to claim that the supply of bid solicitation packages has been exhausted and no more are available. The uninitiated will usually walk away, not realizing that the agency is required by law to supply bid invitations to most interested firms. If the bid package is requested by phone or mail, however, buyocrats can simply delay mailing it out until it is too late for the unwanted contender to respond.

WHAT YOU CAN DO ABOUT IT

Just because a bid is slanted does not mean there is no hope of winning. More than one smart vendor has turned a slanted bid to its advantage and outfoxed a favored contractor. Cutting the price is often a good ploy if you do it without losing your shirt. The favored firm expects to win and usually prices high, so it is vulnerable to a knockout low bid. One program office slanted the bid toward the incumbent vendor by offering a special credit for installed equipment that had been leased, but a shrewd rival offset this by offering a more attractive trade-in deal to replace the installed equipment.

A project office may be so successful in discouraging competition that only one firm bids. The lucky bidder is in a sole-source position and holds most of the trumps in any negotiation. Lack of response clearly indicates a defective bid package. Responsible project offices would consider canceling the bid to draw up a better solicitation to attract more bidders. Too often buyocrats award the contract to the single bidder because this bidder is the one they wanted all along, or they don't want to be bothered with resoliciting bids, or they are afraid they will lose budgeted funds if they don't make an award. When something like this happens, try a protest to higher agency officials or the General Accounting Office (GAO). GAO has ruled both ways, depending on circumstances, approving some awards to single bidders, rejecting others.

THE SECOND TIME AROUND: THE FOLLOW-ON CONTRACT

Most government contracts are for a specified period of time and must be renewed. Each renewal is a new sales opportunity. An incumbent vendor plays many strategies to keep rivals out of the program:

- The incumbent puts very attractively priced follow-on production options in the original contract—for example, sliding scale discounts give the buyer greater and greater cuts the longer the order is continued. A variation is the "all-or-nothing" discount, in which the buyer must complete all production options or lose all discounts.

• The incumbent doesn't contract for any production options at all, but gives a low price on the initial order. After the contract is made, the buyer frequently will not want to change to another vendor immediately for many reasons: interrupted delivery schedules, higher logistic and training costs, risks of going to a new supplier. Thus, after the initial contract order runs out, the buyer comes back to negotiate a follow-on order, which the incumbent vendor can then price high enough to recoup earlier loss and get a tidy profit. This ploy was successfully used for radio navigation sets for Army helicopters.

• The incumbent proposes modifications to upgrade the present product. The agency gives a sole-source contract to develop the upgraded product, and the initial sole-source production contract is extended because the company is the only firm with the knowledge of how to build the new product.

Caution: The firm must be sure it knows its buyer well. Some buyers may take the incumbent's ideas on product modification and put them out for competitive bid.

• If all else fails and follow-on production still goes out for bids, the incumbent can often keep the production lines going through foreign sales. (This is frequently done for military products.) Foreign buyers are usually more interested in getting proven products than in low price and prefer to buy from the incumbent firm. This leads to interesting competition on longstanding products when several previous builders are all vying for foreign orders. As a last resort, the incumbent can simply license a foreign firm and milk the project for more profit this way.

• The incumbent can still get the program back if the newcomer that grabbed it away then stumbles and falls. Agencies will go to great lengths to be sure the newcomer succeeds, as noted, but frequently the firm bombs out despite the government's helping hand. This is the time for the previous vendor to rush back to seek an urgent sole-source award—priced in the company's favor because the agency is under the gun.

WHEN A CONTRACT IS A STEAL: GRABBING
BUSINESS AWAY FROM INCUMBENTS

A good way to jump into government business is simply to take an existing big project away from the incumbent vendor. Agencies are under pressure to seek bids for big production follow-ons to current programs. In these bids, the contracting office provides all the drawings, all the specifications, sample items, and often the tooling and test equipment as well. The new winning vendor must just build the product.

A newcomer who wants to grab away programs like this must plan a strategy years in advance. Companies that start to prepare when the solicitation comes out are doomed to failure. Here are some suggestions:

- Talk to users of the present equipment. Find out problems, weak points in the present gear.

- Get a copy of the present contract, including specifications (under the Freedom of Information Act, the contracting office must provide this). A follow-on production bid should closely follow the present contract.

- Secure a sample of the equipment for examination. Often it is available from government surplus sales.

- Find copies of technical manuals and government reports on the product and check government repair depots to learn service problems.

- Get good intelligence on precisely how large the future production contract will be. It may end up being too small to be worth the expense and bother of preparing a bid. (Don't take the word of procurement offices; they are masters at holding out a big production carrot to encourage bidders to cut their prices.) Find out how much money has been budgeted for anticipated orders, and check the agency comptroller's office or budget officials and friends inside the program office to be sure that the forecast quantities are correct.

You must be a gambler to play this game. Intense competition pushes bid prices to rock-bottom levels. The tipoff should be that the incumbent builder often is among the higher priced bidders.

The incumbent knows the problems involved intimately and puts a high headache factor into the price. The winner of a follow-on production bid with a low price has one good thing going—the possibility of attaining privileged status. Agency necks are on the block. These people will go to great lengths to help the new contract winner build the product, sometimes providing technicians and engineers as well as extra equipment and tooling, and even finding ways to adjust the contract price higher.

Caution: The incumbent vendor is not happy to see a newcomer take over, so the incumbent often gives incomplete drawings or "forgets" to include minor changes to the product that may be critical. Even if an incumbent supplies the most accurate drawings possible, there is often some production-line wizardry, such as making changes in production gear that turns out a working finished product. The newcomer must learn this unspecified art the hard way, because no engineering drawing can convey such production nuances. Often a newcomer underestimates the difficulty of building a new product, even though all the drawings and data are supplied. New contractors must plan to make money on the one production order they managed to grab. It is all too likely that another newcomer will use the same tactics to steal away the next production buy.

THROW OUT A LIFELINE: HOW A PROL
CAN GET IN ON THE SOLE-SOURCE GAME

A good chance for prols and small firms to get business comes when a larger company is in trouble on a project. Often the big firm simply subcontracts the entire job to the small company, sometimes at a higher price than the original contract. A large military radio prime was willing to pay a small firm $600,000 above the original contract award to take over a contract for an aircraft radio that the prime couldn't build. The big firm didn't want to blacken its reputation with a contract termination and was willing to lose money to get help.

Often the small firm is a major supplier to the troubled prime, learns of the difficulties, and can make its unsolicited pitch to take over the problem contract. Sometimes the large prime builds modules and parts but turns to low-cost small firms to complete a fixed-price contract that would end up in red ink if the high-overhead prime tried to finish the work itself.

Big primes also put many small firms into a product line by selling them technology and data rights when the prime is dropping the line. A limited or declining market may be too costly for a high-overhead prime to service, or competition may have bid the price down to levels so low a big firm can no longer make a profit. Smart primes sell their data rights and know-how to a low-overhead smaller firm that can still make money with the product line.

This examination of the world of sole-sourcing may sound negative, but it is real, and there is honest hope for the newcomer. No matter how solidly entrenched a favored firm seems to be with a program office, at any given moment there is a chance that competitors can make inroads into the project in the future. Agency sponsors of the incumbent firm may depart. Agency requirements can change overnight. Sudden budget cuts can make the favored vendor too expensive for the program pocketbook. Whatever the shift in fortunes, alert firms may suddenly find a chance to squeeze into a project long denied to them. A big contractor locked solidly into an Army field computer project gradually found itself losing bits and pieces to competitors over the years. One firm took over input terminals when the incumbent contractor could not deliver units. Two years later, another firm stole the computer peripherals away when it offered far lower prices. Finally, the once-entrenched favorite almost lost everything when another computer firm nearly walked off with the main field computer business.

It is up to the new contractor to go back to the beginning of this chapter; all the moves and countermoves of the sole-source game are now yours to make. Good luck.

5

A BAEDECKER ON BIDS

THE TYPE OF BIDS YOU MEET—AND HOW TO HANDLE THEM:
- Invitation for Bid (IFB)
- Two-step IFB
- IFB with qualified products list
- IFB with bid sample
- Request for Quotation (RFQ)
- Request for Information (RFI)
- Request for Proposal (RFP)
- Other tricky bid types

BID FACTS OF LIFE: AMENDMENTS, BOILERPLATE, STANDARDS

5. A BAEDECKER ON BIDS

Flare Linen Service (not its real name) was asked by the local air base depot to bid on a one-year contract to rent towels and wiping cloths; the previous vendor had gone bankrupt. Flare Linen had never done a nickel's worth of government business, but the owner said, "Why not?" and asked for the bid package. Three months later—it takes time for contract officers to draw up even the simplest solicitation—Flare Linen got a massive folio in the mail, 420 pages of incomprehensible legal jargon and illegible photocopied pages of agate type. The work description of the project was buried somewhere in thirty-seven pages of cryptic forms and law-text clauses. Other specifications involving the job were scattered throughout the package. Flare Linen's chief made a rough guess that he would have to spend ten hours he could ill afford away from his regular duties just to fathom the bid gobbledegook.

At this point many frustrated newcomers just chuck the bid tome into the circular file and forget about the whole project. The Flare Linen executive was so mad he whipped off the entire bid package to his Congressional representative with a sharp note expressing his frustration: "How can the Air Force expect any normal company to wade through such a mass of material just for a one-year contract with very low profit?"

The answer is that more than 100,000 companies suffer through the bid document maze to win government contracts each year. For better or worse, these firms have learned to cope with jargon and ponderous bid forms.

Here's a brief tour guide to wandering through the federal bid wilds. Once you get into the actual situation, you may want to go to more detailed sources for help. But to get you started:

INVITATION FOR BID (IFB)

This is the traditional advertised bid with the low-price-take-all award. In 1977 it was the only standard approved procurement. Any other type of bid or procurement had to be justified as an exception, often with extensive documentation and paperwork. Newcomers to the market often assume IFB is the major way government does business, but they couldn't be more wrong! Only about 16 percent of all contract awards are made through IFB competition.

Many project officers distrust IFB because they have no chance to choose among different features of a proposal. They are forced to take the low price, whether they like the product or not. The chance is great that a firm may "buy in" on the contract by proposing an unrealistically low price just to be sure of getting the award. IFBs require detailed specifications, since the deciding factor is price, not any technical ability or unique product feature. Buyers, often legitimately, want greater flexibility to negotiate different proposals from various qualified vendors. Other buying offices dislike IFBs because they can't write good bid specs and prefer the maneuvering that other bid forms allow for working around fuzzy or incomplete specifications.

IFBs have a stated bid opening date, sometimes only minutes after the deadline for proposals to be turned in. Bidders jam into the bid opening room at the agency. Each contender's sealed bid envelope is opened and the price is announced. The lowest price automatically wins. If that firm then passes an agency pre-award survey on its ability to perform the work, a contract will be signed within weeks or months.

Strategy: If your price was near the low-price bidder's, challenge that firm's competency to do the work, especially if it is a small business. The firm might be judged incapable of performance and the next low price selected for the award. Some IFBs will disqualify three or four low-price small firms before awarding the contract to the next firm in line. If the low-price bidder is a medium to large firm, try to convince the agency contract office that the company is "buying in" with an unreasonable price. Go over the low-price bid with a microscope to find some flaw that might disqualify it. Watch the eventual contract to be sure it corresponds in every way to all the specs and requirements of the IFB. If there is any deviation, you have good grounds for a protest to agency superiors or to the General Accounting Office.

Counterstrategy: If your firm is the low-price bidder, know such challenges may be coming. Document your ability to perform. List suppliers. Provide summaries of plant capability and personnel. Have them ready for the agency pre-award review.

Strategy: IFBs give a firm more advantage over rivals than other types of bids. Fear of newcomers and small firms low-balling the price may keep many larger firms from bidding at all. However, IFBs are a good way for buyocrats to slant a bid for a favored vendor, especially if they write rigid specs exactly around that firm's product or service. (If you suspect a rigged bid, make no bid yourself or protest—both strategies are covered in detail later. See Chapter 12, " 'I've Been Robbed!': The Art of Protesting.")

TWO-STEP IFB

The two-step IFB tries to eliminate some of the disadvantages of the normal IFB. Bidders submit only technical and management proposals first, and only those companies judged technically qualified are allowed to submit price bids on a second step. The award still goes automatically to the low-price bidder, but the theory is that unqualified firms have been eliminated, so any of the finalists should be capable of performing the work.

The so-called "two-stepper" still does not stop "buy-ins." All the rigidity and lack of negotiations inherent in IFBs are still there. In addition, the bid cycle can be held up for prolonged periods while disqualified firms protest their elimination. Agencies may be capricious and arbitrary in disqualifying firms—yet there are few higher authorities in government willing to second-guess the project office's judgment.

Strategy: The original first-step technical proposal must be clearly written and leave no unanswered questions. There will be no negotiations to take care of ambiguities. You get no second chance on a two-step IFB. Many firms, even veteran contractors, mistakenly think that price is everything on an IFB and do a hasty, ill-prepared first step technical proposal, only to find that they never get into the finals for the second-step price proposal.

IFB WITH QUALIFIED PRODUCTS LIST (QPL)

Another wrinkle on the IFB is to require vendors to pass a specific qualifying test before they become eligible to bid on an IFB. Only those firms on the Qualified Products List (QPL) are solicited in the IFB competition. The object again is to prevent incompetent firms—"garage shops," in the jargon of the industry—from buying in on a contract and then never delivering.

Of course, there are continued protests by vendors who cannot get their products qualified. Agencies can be capricious in accepting a firm's product. A leading instrument firm was on a Navy QPL list but was rejected for an Air Force QPL. One of the largest computer keypunch manufacturers was kept off an Air Force QPL on the technicality that the firm did not have "top-secret" security clearance—only "secret"—even though 90 percent of all orders were for unclassified locations. Some buyers do not even publicize the fact that they have Qualified Product Lists—so QPL procurements are a chummy family affair with a few select vendors.

IFB WITH BID SAMPLE

Yet another variation is to require vendors to submit a sample product for testing before they can qualify to submit price quotations. Buying offices are divided on the use of bid samples. Many agencies feel that bid samples do not follow procurement regulation demands to allow free and open competition—after all, a firm must build the product first on its own money before it can even be given a chance to bid. Others swear by bid samples, claiming that they allow an agency to "kick the tires and blow the horn" before making a purchase, the same as any commercial buyer.

> *Strategy:* Presell an agency using QPL or bid samples to grease the wheels for qualifying your product. Promote the product to technical people, laboratory technicians, research officials of the agency. Build support at the ground level so agency buyers and contract officers don't summarily reject the item. Early warning that a bid solicitation is coming out in several months is essential to start adapting a product. It may be too late to qualify a product if the first time you hear of the bid is when a formal IFB is issued.

REQUEST FOR QUOTATION (RFQ)

For contracts under $10,000, program offices may use a more flexible bid exception, called the Request for Quotation (RFQ). The bid solicitation must still spell out in fairly precise terms just what product or service the agency wants. The RFQ is also supposed to be reasonably short, although, as with most federal bid packages, the verbiage of RFQs is growing. In fact, many RFQs are getting so complex that the original purpose of such a bid is lost: a relatively quick and simple bid technique for agency customers to meet their needs. The RFQ does allow contract offices to negotiate with bidders, although this is not mandatory. But if bidders are called in to discuss their proposals, they have a chance to explain their offers and to question program officials to clear up ambiguities. (See Chapter 9, "Negotiations: Where Most Sales Are Really Made.")

Caution: Buyers sometimes use RFQs as a way to award contracts to favored vendors. Unlike the no-deviation-allowed IFB, the RFQ has enough flexibility for buyers to maneuver to select the winner that they wanted all along. The award in an RFQ also does not have to go to the low bidder as in an IFB, giving program officials more latitude. RFQs are supposed to be used only for bids under $10,000, but buyers who want a quick and dirty contract award occasionally use an RFQ for projects of more than $1 million.

REQUEST FOR INFORMATION (RFI)

Many times, agencies are not ready to make an actual procurement, but they want either to survey the market to find vendors who are interested in bidding later, or to educate themselves on technology or products available. Program offices then issue RFIs, and vendors are free to submit information on company capabilities and possible products or just to indicate an interest in receiving the bid solicitation when it comes out.

Caution: Tell a project office only enough to entice them. A firm that submits detailed information may find its ideas and concepts given to competitors. RFIs still cost money to prepare; frequently, the agency wants a broad range of capabilities covered, which requires time-consuming effort to supply. But companies get no funding for answering RFIs. In fact, unscrupulous buyers may try to get concept ideas and planning data free through RFIs, rather than having to fund studies through normal bids.

REQUEST FOR PROPOSAL (RFP)

The RFP is the workhorse of government buying. Negotiated RFPs account for more than 80 percent of all federal procurement. Instead of the IFB sudden-death price opening, an RFP involves many steps. Each contender submits a proposal by the bid deadline. The agency may or may not ask for prices at that time. The agency contract office then calls in one, several, or all contenders to negotiate the contract terms and conditions, work statement, schedules—and ultimately the cost. Bureaucracy is under no mandate to negotiate with bidders. Companies are free to change their proposals and prices during the negotiations. Indeed, the object of negotiations is to clarify any questions asked by either side. After negotiations are completed, a deadline is usually set for all contenders to submit their final prices.

Buyers do not have to award the contract to the low-price bidder under an RFP. Technically, they are free to choose the product judged to best meet the bid requirements, even if it may have the highest bid price. That opens a Pandora's box of protests and controversy, as low-price bidders who were passed over object vigorously. When a contract is awarded on factors other than low price, the subjective judgment of the agency is challenged by all losers.

Negotiations themselves are often prolonged, costly exercises. There is always the danger that one firm's prices and technical features may be leaked deliberately or inadvertently to other contenders during highly detailed sessions.

RFPs can also use the two-step process, QPL, or bid samples—with all the attendant problems and opportunities already examined.

Since RFP is the predominant form of government buying, the questions, quandaries, and quixotic episodes that plague RFP procurements from proposal writing to contract award and afterward will occupy most of the rest of this book. Many of the problems are also encountered in other types of bids. Only a step-by-step review of the process will help you make any sense out of this world of jargon.

OTHER TRICKY BID TYPES

Not to be straitjacketed by the more traditional bid forms, agencies have a variety of other solicitation techniques, many of them frequently abused to slant awards to favorite firms.

The Telephone Solicitation. This is supposed to be used only for small purchases. The dollar amount varies agency by agency but is generally from under $5000 to $10,000. For a speedy bid the project office is allowed to telephone a number of vendors for a price quotation on a specific piece of equipment or service. There's no set rule on how many vendors or just which firms must be called, so buyers usually telephone only a handful of companies they know. Vendors often don't know precisely what the project office wants, and telephone conversations are subject to error and misinterpretation. In many cases, the telephone solicitation is merely a subterfuge for giving a sole source to a favorite contractor. Competitors who suspect foul play should protest immediately to agency superiors, the GAO, or their representative in Congress. A protest made after the contract is awarded is often too late—shrewd buyocrats cover their tracks enough to justify the award.

The Telegraphic Bid. Soliciting bids by telex or telegram is slightly better than telephone solicitation because the bid request is at least in writing. But again, only a small number of "in" contractors are solicited; outsiders or firms the program office doesn't want never learn of the bid until it is too late. Telegraphic bids often have such a short response deadline that only a few firms can reply. This bid type also is a pet way for buyocrats to wire in a contract for a favored firm.

ADDITIONS AND SUBTRACTIONS:
FAST FIGURING FOR BIDDERS

Agency program officials are inveterate mind-changers. It is a rare major bid—or even minor procurement—that does not have a string of amendments, changes, and modifications during the bid cycle. Many changes are mundane but still spoil any attempt at orderly proposal writing because the firm must analyze and respond to each amendment telexed from the program office. Some changes are metamorphic, transforming the project under bid into an entirely new program. Frequently, major recasting amendments drop on bidders just before the bid deadline, after firms have spent countless hours and a great deal of money preparing elaborate proposals for the original solicitation. Now they must start back at ground zero to draw up an almost entirely new proposal to meet the revamped bid. Companies can often write off some share of their proposal efforts on other government contracts but still end up eating a large share of the cost for buyocratic mind-changing themselves.

> *Caution:* Prols and small firms must be especially careful to keep track of frequent and varied bid amendments. An incumbent firm providing laundry service to an Army base lost the bid for the next three years' service because a crucial amendment arrived in the mail while the company president was ill. No one else in the small firm spotted it. Result: The firm failed to respond to a mandatory new penalty clause, and its bid was thrown out as nonresponsive.

Uncle Sam addeth—and Uncle Sam taketh away in bid solicitations. Especially galling to bidders are last-minute amendments slashing order quantities. Firms might never have bothered to prepare a proposal had they known a program office was going to buy such a small amount. But if buyocrats wait until only days before the bid deadline to cut quantities, vendors may already have made a major proposal effort.

> *Caution:* During later bid negotiations on an RFP, one contender may convince the agency program office that a significant change—in design, operation, scheduling, costs—should be made, deviating from specifications and conditions in the bid solicitation. If the project office accepts the change, legally they must amend the RFP to allow other firms to respond to the same modification. Sometimes buyers, intentionally or by mistake, fail to amend the RFP and award a contract on the altered concept. This provides losers with one of their best chances of winning a protest to the GAO to overturn the award. (See Chapter 12, " 'I've Been Robbed!': The Art of Protesting.")

> *Caution:* Bid amendments are often a sure tipoff that a favored vendor has gotten agency powers to adopt his concept. Buying offices follow the letter of the law and amend the RFP to allow other firms to respond to the altered bid, but they have already made up their minds to go with the vendor who first suggested the change. Sometimes other firms can try to trump the likely winner by lowering their

price. A blatant bid amendment adopting one firm's exclusive product features can be protested. Even if the protest is not successful, it may drag out the procurement until the project office changes its mind again and comes out with an entirely new bid.

BID BOILERPLATE: A FACT OF LIFE

A feature common to almost every type of federal bid is "boilerplate." The term comes from old-time county weekly newspapers, which used reams of syndicated "boilerplate" stories and features to fill up the paper. Boilerplate reaches its epitome in government bids: hundreds and thousands of standard, preprinted pages containing every conceivable term and condition. Bids for even the simplest product may be 80 percent boilerplate clauses. A Labor Department bid for part-time editing of one of its magazines contained two pages concerning the actual work and seventy-two pages of boilerplate (including eleven pages requiring adherence to the Clean Air and Water Act). An Army bid for a $400 voltmeter had 192 pages of boilerplate; disgusted contracting officials estimated that this cost the Army more in paperwork than the entire value of the instruments themselves.

Boilerplate is the buyocrat's security blanket. Project officials load up the bid package with every possible standard term and condition to protect themselves from every problem that could arise in the eventual contract, so that whatever trouble erupts, they can say they tried to head it off by including an appropriate boilerplate demand in the original bid package. This can lead to absurd cases: a bid for a new airplane contained boilerplate clauses on humane slaughter of livestock. Many boilerplate clauses are required by law. The more politicians try to correct procurement problems by passing new laws, the more boilerplate is stapled onto every federal bid solicitation.

Often so much boilerplate is dumped into an IFB or an RFP that only the largest primes have enough lawyers and contract specialists to cope with the mountains of clauses and terms. Even they can get tripped up by simple boilerplate conditions that they overlook. The little firm, the newcomer, the unwary vendor may be forced to just gamble that agencies will not enforce all boilerplate clauses if the firm should get into trouble. Of course, many of the standard clauses become old hat as vendors run into them in bid package after bid package.

> *Caution:* Small wording changes can be made in boilerplate clauses that veteran contractors gloss over because they are so familiar. A company bid proposal costing thousands of dollars to prepare can be thrown out for not meeting some obscure demand. If the firm does win the contract, company officials may be surprised to find that they have agreed to weird boilerplate conditions in the bid package. Boilerplate booby traps may not surface until far into the contract performance, when government auditors examining contractor books suddenly discover that the firm failed to meet conditions they hadn't ever considered. The Air Force terminated a microwave communication network it was building in the Middle East but refused to pay travel costs back to the United States for 750 employees on the project. The Air Force said a boilerplate clause exempted such costs—so the unfortunate firm was forced to pay high relocation costs for its workers on top of losing the contract.

The mass of boilerplate runs up the cost of preparing bids astronomically. Firms must employ legions of engineers, lawyers, technical writers, and clerical help to answer countless boilerplate questions. Eventually, Uncle Sam pays much of this cost. The contract winner charges off the expense as part of the contract; the losers all charge off part of the cost on other government contracts. But rather than reduce boilerplate to cut costs, bureaucracy seems bent on throwing more and more conditions into bid packages, for reasons already detailed. The taxpayer, who probably has never seen a bulging federal bid, ends up footing the boilerplate bill. Nothing is likely to stop the paper avalanche until agencies themselves are motivated to cut back. And this will come only when agency budgeters refuse to let program offices build empires by adding paper shufflers to process boilerplate clauses.

STANDARDS: THE STANDARD OPERATING PROCEDURE ON BIDS

Almost as pervasive as boilerplate is the mass of government standards and general specifications. A few may be spelled out in detail, but as many as forty to fifty different government standards and specs included in the bid document may simply be cited by name, and the bidder is expected to know the full details. Worse yet, any one standard may include as many as twenty to thirty other allied standards. It is not uncommon for a routine bid to cover more than 100 standards, cited by name, and including other standards incorporated in them by reference. The Department of Defense alone has 40,000 different standards to choose from. These standards are often hopelessly complex and verbose. The Pentagon has a five-page standard just for chewing gum.

Big contractors hire offices of technicians just to follow major government standards and specifications. The small firm does well to know just a few major standards; it cannot hope to become intimate with the thousands of standards in the government bag. Many small companies simply gamble, hoping the procuring agency will overlook minor deviations or will help the firm meet the requirements. Some small companies have found it quite possible to become knowledgeable on a few standards common to one product they make. Small firms can also hire a limited number of experts to follow key standards affecting them just as they hire legal, technical, and accounting talent. A prol can even turn the federal standard maze to its advantage by specializing in meeting one type of standard and even helping primes and privileged firms to meet that spec. One firm with twenty employees built a nice business doing specialized high-reliability product testing. Large firms paid for the unique testing services rather than trying to meet the reliability testing standard themselves.

Some typical standards headaches:

- Standards vary from agency to agency. Just when weary vendors think they have mastered the major federal standards, they confront entirely new ones in another agency's bid solicitation. Part of the problem: Everyone wants their own standards and doesn't trust anyone else's. Many are nearly the same—agencies merely adapt and change them to fit their own whims. Federal authorities have long tried to get agencies to adopt uniform standards for bids, but it takes years just to get agreement on a few minor points, and by that time feuding agencies have dreamed up new sets of standards and specifications.

- Many standards are out of date. By the time one is adopted, technology or events have made it hopelessly obsolete. Many times Uncle Sam is stuck with an aged standard simply because it is the best available. Thousands of standards pass into the bureaucratic graveyard but still may show up in bid packages by reference or incorporation into another standard. Even the Feds have trouble trying to weed out obsolete standards. Pity the poor contractor who tries to keep up with current developments.

· Standards can be anticompetitive—either by accident or by deliberate ploy. They may be so tough that only a very few firms can master the specs. The National Security Agency standard for eliminating any signal emission outside of a product is so stringent that only a handful of firms can pass and qualify for tens of millions of dollars of business. Belatedly, buyers recognize how standards can thwart competition, and some give vendors a grace period to pass strict standards tests. Sometimes agencies will even fund winning firms to help them meet exceedingly harsh standards.

A final word on bids: try to read every part. You never know what innocent-looking clause may sink you later. If you don't understand what the language means—and this is quite probable— find someone who can interpret it, whether it is the agency, a trade association, a consultant, or a contract specialist on your staff. As in mastering a foreign language, the more bid gobbledegook you plow through, the more proficient you become at interpreting it.

A small Massachusetts laboratory likes the bid jargon. "It scares away scores of potential competitors," says the company president, happy to have the field almost completely open on some bids. Be wary, but don't let federal bids frighten you away from business that could be yours.

6

TO BID OR NOT TO BID: THAT IS THE QUESTION

•NINE BASIC QUESTIONS A BIDDER SHOULD ANSWER
BEFORE GOING AHEAD WITH THE MAJOR EFFORT
OF PREPARING A PROPOSAL

6. TO BID OR NOT TO BID: THAT IS THE QUESTION

A company's smartest bid may be the one it doesn't make.

Proposals are expensive. Responding to even the simplest bid solicitation may cost a firm tens of thousands of dollars, counting legal, financial, and technical review of the mass of government boilerplate and careful review of the special requirements of the specific bid. Large firms have dropped as much as a million dollars of their own funds preparing for large, complex defense bids. Since no company can make a business of just answering RFPs or IFBs, a firm must be sure it has a reasonable chance to win the competition.

How can a company avoid blind alleys and wasted effort? When is a vendor probably better off not bidding? Some guidelines:

1. *Has Your Company Done Its Homework?* Has it spent months beforehand working with all levels of the agency to see what user needs are? Has the firm gotten enough advance dope on what will be included in an upcoming bid so that it has been preparing its proposal months before the RFP came out? Entrenched rivals most certainly have been working the agency long before the bid solicitation. If a firm starts its bid response when it receives the official RFP, it's probably too late.

2. *Is This a "Real" Bid that Is Meeting an Actual Need?* As previously outlined, agencies resort to smokescreen bids to meet political pressure by a show of activity. Such phantom projects have little solid base and often blow away as soon as political attention is diverted elsewhere.

Many project offices bother industry with needless bids; they are just testing the market, much as Sunday house-shoppers peruse the real estate market. Companies invest large sums of money in responding to such bids, only to find that no contract is ever awarded. At best, only limited study contracts are signed, a far cry from huge buying quantities forecast in the original RFP.

Also, project offices all too frequently go out for bids before they have budget funds committed. Buyers desperately hope they will get money approved by the time bidders turn in proposals. Yet budgets are often snarled in red tape or bickering. Contracts are never awarded—or suffer year-long delays after vendors have responded in good faith.

Strategy: Good intelligence on agency budgets is critical. Friends in the comptroller's office can tell you whether the project office really has funds committed or is merely "betting on the come." Many large projects must be approved at various higher levels within an agency. Checking with these higher offices should indicate whether or not a project has approved funding.

3. *How Well Does the Customer Know Your Company?* Is the project office aware of your firm's previous work and capabilities? Has the company psyched decision-makers in the agency? Do you know their prejudices, quirks, desires? Since scores of agency officials get their hands into the bid soup, a vendor does well to scout out as many executives as possible. Major contractors employ legions of marketers to carry their gospel through agencies. But smaller primes can sell themselves if they zero in on a few projects with highest potential payoff, rather than trying to spread themselves too thin covering an agency entirely. Prols have no chance to sell themselves, since by definition they are the drones of the procurement world. Their best chance is to find the project office that buys on price alone and then fight it out on price alone. Fortunately, such offices abound in government, giving life and hope to countless prols.

4. *Is the RFP or IFB Itself Defective?* Government bid solicitations have plenty of pitfalls, as we have seen, and a firm does well to avoid or neutralize such bid sand traps. However, some bid packages are so defective that a company should seriously consider not bidding at all. It would take encyclopedias to detail all possible bid solicitation dangers, but some of the most common red flags are:

Criteria for evaluating proposals are not given or are vague and ambiguous. A firm is foolish to invest heavily to prepare a bid if it doesn't know what yardstick will be used to judge its proposal. The project office can use any basis to pick a winner—perhaps a favorite it wanted all along.

The bid document does not define how long a life cycle is planned for the products or services being acquired. This is crucial when the customer is going to lease or rent equipment. If lifetime is not spelled out, contenders can play bidding tricks, offering free rental for some months to get extra evaluation credit.

The RFP or IFB does not define maintenance needs. This opens the bid to trick maintenance offers that may win the contract for a firm, but may never be exercised by the agency.

The bid document ignores related but high-stake costs. Will the agency pay for special features, manuals, training, transportation, site preparation? Ignoring such factors when a million dollars may be at stake is asking for trouble.

Acceptance test conditions are vague, unfair, too strict, or faulty. The RFP may call for an elaborate benchmark test— to pass, you must spend hundreds of thousands of dollars to prepare for the test.

The product specs may be so unclear in the RFP or IFB that no one knows what the project office really wants. The buyer may end up trying to evaluate proposals as widely disparate as dogs and dinosaurs. A firm may even win such a poorly specified bid, only to find it cannot build the product called for. A friendly buyocrat may bail a firm out of such a quandary, but many rigid project offices try to enforce unworkable specs.

Expected award date is not given, leaving firms with investments of time and money and wondering whether to hold on to staff.

5. Is the Customer Asking Bidders to Assume Too Much Risk? Is the project office trying to buy a never-before-built, complex product on a fixed-price contract? Suppliers would be well advised to shun such bids unless they are assured that a friendly agency will bail them out if they run into cost problems.

Does the agency insist on a high-liability clause and risky liquidated damage clauses? Some sporty competitors don't mind gambling on such high-risk contract clauses. They calculate that the government will not bankrupt their firms by enforcing astronomical damages that might conceivably occur. But Uncle Sam is no different from any other contract holder who expects the terms of the pact to be met. The best rule: Be prepared to live with what you bid. If you can't, don't bid.

6. *Is the Bid Wired in for a Favored Vendor?* As we've seen, a main ploy of buyocrats and vendors alike is to slant bid specifications or terms so that only a favorite firm can emerge the winner. Rivals who drop a lot of company funds preparing proposals in such biased bids are usually throwing their money away.

Even the largest contractors get suckered into bidding on projects that are predestined to go to an agency favorite. Often overly optimistic marketing managers—or desperate ones—ignore telltale signs. Many company officials think they can beat the odds. A few succeed. Most others must invent last-minute explanations for their top management when they do not.

You should suspect that a bid is wired in for a rival when it has:

A very short deadline—only days or weeks—to turn in a proposal or a very short delivery schedule that few firms, probably only the favored vendor, can meet.

Extra credit given for equipment already installed, favoring the incumbent vendor. Even if such credit is not spelled out in the RFP, guard against the incumbent offering tricky deals to get such evaluation credit to keep the gear installed.

A demand in the RFP to bid all of a wide range of equipment, or to service products on a worldwide basis, or seeking special features not widely available. Any such RFP or IFB clauses suspiciously point toward a vendor that the agency already has in mind.

Special tests required, indicating bias toward one particular vendor.

Product specs that come straight from one manufacturer's data sheet.

7. *Is the Company Willing to Put in Another $10,000 to $100,000 in Extra Bidding Effort?* Too many firms see only the cost of the original proposal—often astronomically high itself—without allowing for the extra money that may be needed in the home stretch. If a firm cannot go the extra mile, it may well want to bow out early in the game.

Also, a firm must be prepared to wait out a long-delayed agency selection process, which can run up high costs in keeping proposal and technical teams together, keeping factory space reserved, and keeping subcontractors on the hook. Contenders may plan on a three- to six-month bid cycle, based on projections of the program office, only to find the bid evaluation dragging on for a year or more. Only firms willing to stick it out should bid in the first place.

8. *Is the Agency Setting up a Glorified Price Auction?* Is the project office asking for several rounds of price bidding—a clear sign that it is pitting contenders against each other in a price bludgeoning? In negotiations, do project officers infer that an extra 5 to 10 percent price cut is expected? Has the agency hinted that it already has one very low bid price from another contender? Is the bid open to all comers with no attempt to qualify any contenders on their technical competence? Is the agency asking bidders to price the cost of building to government-provided engineering drawings, which will attract inexperienced firms attempting to win with only a very low price? Does the project office have a long history of running price auctions?

A vendor may want to jump into such a price fray and punch it out. But if the game plan calls for pricing the bid to assure an adequate profit return, then a company may well be leary of such obvious donnybrooks. Incumbent suppliers often no-bid such price auctions—they know better than everyone else the true costs of making the product, which they cannot recover in a price shootout.

9. *Does the Project Fit in with Company Plans?* Is it a pet idea pushed by the engineering department? Does the firm actually have the resources to perform the contract if it wins? Can it acquire equipment, tooling, talent? At what cost?

Such bid or no-bid decisions seem obvious, yet surprisingly, even the largest contractors get carried away by the glamor of a particular bid and bite off more than they can digest. The marketing department of one of the largest instrument firms in the country steamrollered its management into aggressively bidding a giant multiyear Air Force contract for test equipment for fear that its chief competitor would get the business. No one considered the problems the firm would have if it won, which it did: a drastic shuffling of production schedules to meet the peaks and valleys of erratic Air Force orders, extra training for new workers, new tooling, borrowing of extra capital that could not be charged off to the government, disruption in deliveries to other customers. The unlucky winner bid a price that allowed only a razor-thin profit margin, which was quickly eaten up by the unexpected expenses. However, the feared competitor was smarter. Management saw the hidden expenses and bid the firm's regular catalog price. Any time a vendor bids its regular list price with no discount this is essentially a no-bid (unless the vendor knows that the bid is locked up against all comers).

A vendor has several options in addition to just walking away from a bad bid. Before abdicating, a firm should at least try to change some of the objectionable bid features. Results may be surprising. Sometimes a project office will amend its RFP or IFB to take out onerous demands. Of course, a firm must have some hope that determined agency officials will not simply award the contract to a favored vendor anyway—after cleaning up the bid documents.

Above all else, complain—and early in the bid cycle. Sometimes the project office itself will recognize the defects pointed out and amend its RFP or IFB. Often pressure must be brought at a higher level of the agency or within the parent cabinet-level department.

If complaints within the agency or department fail, file a pre-award protest with GAO. Federal procurement rules forbid slanting RFPs or IFBs to any one supplier, although clever buyocrats have learned to evade such rules with disguised bid specifications. Still, a protest to GAO puts a legal spotlight on the bid solicitation package, and frequently it cannot stand up to such scrutiny. A protest before the contract is awarded has far greater chance of success than a similar protest after the contract has been signed with another firm. Once a contract is awarded, an agency has a wide range of ploys to fend off protests. (See Chapter 12, " 'I've Been Robbed!': The Art of Protesting.")

Or look for a loophole in the bid document that you can twist to your advantage. Not all wired-in bids go to the favored vendor. A few imaginative contenders find unique clauses or terms in the RFP or IFB that can be used to leapfrog the favorite firm. An Army solicitation gave very high evaluation credit for leased computers when title passed to the government—an obvious ploy to slant the bid to the incumbent vendor. But a rival turned the tables by bidding high lease rates for a limited number of months and then gave the computers to the Army title-free, getting enough credit to win the award.

Many firms try for a piece of the action as subcontractors rather than fighting a bad bid package. If the bid is wired in for another firm, a rival can often get large subcontract funding by joining with the favorite rather than fighting it. If bid specifications and terms make it risky to bid as a prime, a subcontract deal with another firm willing to take the gamble may bring in money without the headaches.

> *Caution:* When going the subcontract route, be sure the prime contractor does not pass down all the onerous terms and conditions in the original award to you.

More and more vendors are respectfully declining to bid on huge contracts. A GAO survey of 138 typical bids found a total of 8956 firms invited to bid and only 716 responding. Some bids get only two proposals. Many do not get a single response. Agencies have tried to offset the declining number of bidders by force-feeding—inviting more and more firms to bid. Some procurements have solicited more than 100 firms on a single bid, with less than half a dozen responses.

Each vendor must judge for itself whether to no-bid. This may be the most crucial decision the firm makes in any government procurement.

7

PROPOSAL BOOBY TRAPS
How to Pick Your Way
Carefully

• WHY FEDERAL BUYERS THROW SOME PROPOSALS OUT
RIGHT AT THE START

• PROPOSAL PLANNING: GETTING IT ALL TOGETHER

• THE THREE MAJOR PROPOSALS AND WHAT GOES INTO THEM:
Technical proposal
Management proposal
Cost proposal

• WHAT TO DO IF YOU MAKE A MISTAKE

7. PROPOSAL BOOBY TRAPS
How to Pick Your Way Carefully

One of the nation's largest defense contractors spent $240,000 preparing its complex proposal for a big Air Force RFP for military radars. Since the firm had built earlier radars of this type for the Air Force, it expected to be among the bid finalists. To the shock of everyone on the account from president to marketing manager, the firm's proposal was thrown out early in the bid cycle. "We simply blew it," the firm's marketing veep said later. "We didn't write a good proposal. It was full of holes. We should have known better; there is no excuse."

Proposals for government bids are easy to flub. There are many complexities and many chances for error, and bid deadlines are often short. So many parts of a company and so many different strategies are involved that even giant primes can go awry. A firm may also have several proposal efforts going at any one time—as many as twenty or more for larger firms—and management has trouble giving adequate attention to each. This is a mistake because proposals are expensive, costing the firm anywhere from $50,000 to $1 million or more, and it pays for bidders to put their best foot forward if they are going to make the effort at all.

A proposal, after all, is the firm's major sales pitch to the customer. It can be a binding legal document, since all follow-on negotiations stem directly from it. Your proposal may be the only contact that scores of government technical and management evaluators have with your company. You may never meet these people, but your chance at hundreds of thousands of future sales dollars rests on their interpretation and understanding of your written proposal.

No single chapter, not even an entire library, could detail all there is to know about proposal writing. Each IFB or RFP dictates its own particular approach. Complexities are so great that a company should engage plenty of expertise, either on its own staff or through consultants or experienced sales representatives.

Industry associations, universities, and the government itself run training programs on proposal writing. These vary widely in usefulness, but every firm needs more than just a nuts-and-bolts tutorial. In the real world, management can be blown out by booby traps never covered by the textbooks.

Bidders erroneously assume that the buyers are looking at proposals positively for products, services, and ideas to meet contract needs. But buyers' first pass at bidder responses is largely negative: let's get rid of all the proposals we can. The more proposals eliminated in the early stages of the bid cycle, the simpler the evaluation. Evaluation by elimination is especially prevalent in bids in which agencies already have a favored vendor in mind.

Bidders often make such sudden-death eliminations easy for government evaluators by simple mistakes, like failing to sign a bid. Be sure to sign all forms, bid amendments, drawings—when in doubt, sign it. Another mistake is not answering all mandatory questions, some of which can easily be overlooked, with hundreds of complex forms and blanks scattered throughout the massive RFP. Bidders might also fail to submit the required number of copies, put down the wrong model number for any one of a hundred different major components, or fail to give a definite delivery date. Proposals have been thrown out simply for assuring "earliest possible delivery" with no date specified. If the bid calls for any samples to be supplied, be sure all items match precisely the make and model spelled out in the proposal. One tableware supplier lost a $142,000 contract because he submitted one different knife among thirty-six utensil samples detailed in the written proposal.

Bidders give agencies a good excuse to throw out proposals when they impose extra contract terms and conditions beyond those called for in the IFB or RFP. A firm may offer optional extra terms and conditions subject to later negotiation, but it cannot make its bid contingent upon the agency accepting such demands.

Contenders must respond to every single requirement of the RFP, even the most absurd ones. If a bidder feels that a particular demand is outrageous or faulty, it can suggest alternative approaches as options, but such alternatives may never be considered if the firm has not first answered the mandatory bid requirements. Some vendors deliberately gamble on proposals they know will be nonresponsive, hoping the program office will come to its senses on ludicrous RFP requirements and remove them in later bid amendments, thus making the firm's proposal responsive.

Prols and some low-level primes are especially vulnerable to evaluation by elimination. The safest course for a project office not wishing to award a contract to an unknown vendor is simply to reject the vendor's bid on technicalities. Companies on the low end of the bidding totem pole usually must send in letter-perfect proposals. Of course, a buyer who wants a bargain-basement price often overlooks legal small points that would disqualify a vendor on a different bid. The trick for prols is to know what ground rules the agency is using.

The government bid document may be bad in many places—and could be a complete washout. Don't try to rewrite a bad bid solicitation. You can't win. First, project offices don't want to be told that they can't write decent bid documents, even if they can't. Second, they may feel that they have designed the perfect product or system. Even if wiser industry heads suspect it won't work, they score no points proving this in the proposal.

Badly written IFBs and RFPs cause plenty of heartburn. Bidders often must guess at what the buyer really wants. Specifications, engineering drawings, or work descriptions may be so ambiguous that at best the bidder may propose inadequate hardware or services. At worst, the bidder's proposal on such a vague bid is accepted, and the firm must live with the contract.

Overconfidence often sabotages a proposal. "We have this bid won; let's put our second team on it" can be disastrous. More than one vendor has been shocked to lose a sure thing to a competitor that went all out on a first-rate proposal effort. Other snares: "We've already won three times this year with the program manager on this project—we don't have to worry"; or "We have an inside agent on the evaluation team, so we've got it made." Such misplaced confidence is no substitute for a well-conceived proposal. Marketing managers relying on such strategies alone should be prepared to explain to the boss why the company lost a sure bid.

Equally dangerous is the strategy of just putting in a proposal that is good enough to survive initial agency review and get the firm into the competitive range of bid finalists. Then the firm places the price low to try to walk off with the contract. Such ploys sometimes work, as we have seen, but the risk is high that an inadequate proposal will be tossed out in the initial review. An allied pitfall is assuming that agency evaluation teams never read all of a massive proposal. Rejected bidders learn to their dismay that most government evaluators do plow through all the verbiage.

Proposal writing is a lot like publishing a book. A successful bidder is really a hopeful author. Each good proposal has a title page, a table of contents, an introduction, several chapters, tables and charts, drawings and illustrations, reference material, summaries, appendixes, indexes, and definitions of all terms. All the steps in publishing a book are involved in the process, such as layout, editing, graphics, and reviews. Most proposals are in a binder of some type and look like books. Some are more like encyclopedias, with volumes of material.

Caution: Some bidders get so carried away with the book idea that they prepare artistic masterpieces that fail miserably to respond to the basic RFP. Competence in the mechanics of preparing a proposal cannot cover up any lack of substance in the proposal itself. While bidders want as clean and readable a proposal as possible, the document must be substantive, too.

Bidders must schedule proposal writing as carefully as they schedule a complex production job. A proposal manager divides responsibility for the various parts of the proposal among the proper divisions of the company—engineering, legal, administrative, production, accounting, purchasing—and then orchestrates their input to produce a finished volume. Management manuals outline idealized flowcharts for keeping all parts of the proposal effort working in tandem, and some control system is obviously needed if any finished proposal is to come out. However, practice and theory can differ widely.

Rarely can a contractor get all parts of the company working together perfectly. Overworked department managers must try to work in proposal efforts on top of other corporate emergencies. All departmental contributors are writing and rewriting up to the last minute, often precluding any extensive final review that books say must be done.

Just trying to get it all together within the company can be torturous enough without the confusion wrought by frequent and sudden amendments to the IFB or the RFP from the agency contract office. Many agencies just can't keep from tampering with bid documents, adding goodies here, subtracting requirements there.

Often the original document was so poorly drawn that it must be altered constantly just to get meaningful proposals at all. A favorite ploy of bureaucrats is starting the bid by asking for the moon and then gradually scaling down requirements even before proposals are received in order to get a product or service they can afford.

All this can wreak havoc with the most carefully laid proposal writing plan. Entire sections must be thrown out at the last minute. Vast new chapters must be rushed together within weeks. The chance for error is great in the frantic preparation. Yet the very buyers who caused this frenzy by last-minute bid amendments can be ruthless in rejecting proposals for mistakes.

Except for the simplest IFBs, bidders do not submit one proposal. Even the simplest RFP usually calls for at least three proposals—technical, management, and cost. Contenders may have even more proposals if they submit alternatives. Often, because different parts of the company are preparing these various proposals, they are uneven, disjointed, perhaps even conflicting. Just putting them all under the same cover does not create a unified approach in answer to an RFP.

Whatever else a vendor includes in the proposal, it should contain an executive summary. This key section gives an overview of all the parts of the proposal, summarizing the major information and details. It outlines the program scope, expected results, state of the art, and how work will be accomplished. It summarizes the company experience, program staff, and resources. The executive summary should make explicit reference to the other parts of the proposal, and each theme should be documented and presented in detail. Finally, it should end up with the sales pitch: the reasons why the firm should be awarded the contract.

Some of the common pitfalls in preparing the three basic proposals follow.

TECHNICAL PROPOSAL

  · Letting the engineering department run amok. Avoid the technical symposium approach. The customer may not understand pages of equations and technical minutia. Bidders may get a chance in subsequent bid negotiations to explain their technical approach, but firms start off in a bad position if agencies don't grasp the concept immediately from the proposal. Don't count on negotiations to untangle technical confusion. Discussions can be cut short. Many of the customer's misunderstandings may never come up.

- Writing a Ph.D. dissertation rather than a readable sales presentation in simple English. This does not mean that government evaluators reviewing proposals are not learned, but technical experts from many fields are called in by the agency, and terminology that is well known in one technical branch may be less familiar to other specialists. Besides, a technical proposal is still a sales pitch, no matter how detailed it must be. Why make it difficult for the customer to read what you are trying to say? Include a nontechnical synopsis of each highly technical part of the proposal so that nonengineering members of the government negotiating team will understand your concept.

- Forgetting that government evaluators don't keep engineering dictionaries at their elbows while reviewing your proposal. Define all terms used.

- Looking at all technical solutions through rose-colored glasses. Assign degrees of technical risk to various approaches. Show ways to minimize risk. Unless the agency wants to be kidded into "No problem developing this," it wants an idea of the risk involved in any selected concept. Knowledgeable purchasers have probably done their own homework to come up with ideas of the risks involved. The Department of Defense and some other agencies may negotiate higher profits on high-risk contracts; it is in the bidder's own self-interest to assess such risks in proposals.

- Failing to document reliability data for proposed technical approaches. Detailed reliability figures for proven components and subsystems give some idea of estimated reliability for the overall system. Detailed production plans, quality control plans, and anticipated reliability tests can back up the proposal's claims for overall system reliability.

- Slipping up in detailed data on facilities to be used, equipment needs, program schedules, labor requirements, test equipment, and procedures.

- Failing to detect potential trouble spots in specifications, engineering drawings, standards, or work statements in the bid solicitation. The most innocent omission can come back to haunt you if you win the contract. If work is to be done at a government-directed site, visit the location to know what you are getting into. An excavator who failed to inspect an unusually rocky terrain before submitting a proposal was denied any later contract relief for high costs of digging through layers of granite.

- Omitting a list of potential subcontractors by name and experience. The technical proposal does not bind you to using any listed subcontractor should you win the contract, although you face some hard justification to the agency if you try to switch to other sources after the contract is signed.

- Ignoring maintenance, logistics, ease of repair.

Special considerations and alternate technical approaches can be both a plus and a minus. Agencies are fond of urging bidders to recommend optional technical concepts, but bidders often spend considerable time drawing up imaginative alternatives that bring no return. Generally, a program office must award a contract strictly on the basis of specs in the RFP; simply jumping to one firm's alternate proposal without giving others a chance to respond to that idea could violate bid regulations. Thus, alternate proposals, like unsolicited proposals, often end up being sent out to all bidders as an RFP amendment. Ideally, the firm originating the alternative idea is in the strongest position to beat out rivals, but there is no guarantee. You may end up giving a competitor a technical concept it had never considered, which it then uses to knock you out of the bid.

Sometimes a friendly program office may not expose your alternate proposal to rivals but will award the contract with modifications and changes to reach the same alternative concept. Some RFPs specifically invite alternate ideas, making company proposal writing and government evaluation a sporty business. It opens competition to a Ouija board selection among a wide range of vastly different proposals.

Bidders may be asked to support technical proposal claims by submitting bid samples or by passing benchmark tests. Bid samples are supposed to allow the customer to kick the tires and check out all claims. These samples may not have to fulfill bid specifications exactly but must demonstrate the bidder's ability to build requested hardware. This practice is often abused by program offices that already have a few favored vendors in mind and want to lock out uncertain suppliers. Bid samples with unusual or costly features can be demanded so that only a few firms can qualify. Testing of bid samples opens a Pandora's box of disputes: rejected bidders may charge unfair or inadequate government testing or leaks to competitors.

Strategy: Know your customer. If the customer is using bid samples to lock out unwanted vendors, it may not be worth the high cost of adapting equipment to meet the sample specs. Try to get agency superiors, superagency officials, or Congressional power leaders to bring pressure to open up bid sample specs to greater competition. GAO and SBA usually have little power in this area.

Similar caution should be exercised when the government specifies benchmark tests, qualifying hardware tests, or demonstrations. Uncle Sam may foot the bill for a few of the most costly test programs, but most pre-award testing to support a technical proposal is at bidder expense. Agencies may not set adequate tests that truly reflect bid requirements. This hurts the conscientious bidder who struggles to meet bid specs, not concentrating on the test or demonstration. The winner puts all its funds into passing the tests and worries later about meeting contract specs.

Caution: Bidders can assemble teams of costly talent to run benchmark tests and then wait indefinitely for the tests, which are continually postponed. Expenses mount. Companies can rarely recover such costs; competitive pressure keeps most from raising bid prices enough to fully recover the expenses of testing delays.

MANAGEMENT PROPOSAL

- Failing to give as much attention to the management of a project as to the technical details. More than one bidder that was rated highest for its technical proposal has lost the contract because of a poor management proposal. Small firms headed by engineers often concentrate on the technology of a project and miss the importance of convincing the customer that they can manage the program as well.

- Overlooking ways to sell the company's expertise. Include personnel resumés of officers and key employees who will be involved in the project. Detail the company's past performance, facilities, accounting systems, policies, financial resources, and capitalization.

- Failing to highlight the particular management control programs in vogue at the moment with the agency— configuration management, value engineering, you name it.

- Skimping on detailed plans for equal opportunity employment and subcontracting to small and minority businesses. An aerospace contractor lost a $10 million project because NASA ruled that a competitor offered a better plan to bring more minority businesses into the program.

- Omitting detailed data on logistics, training, and engineering support.

- Failing to respond to any of the hundreds of boilerplate terms and conditions demanded in the bid document. Many times the boilerplate can simply be signed and attached to the firm's proposal. Some boilerplate may have blanks that are to be filled in by bidders; be sure all requested data have been written in.

COST PROPOSAL

- Failing to document cost estimates adequately. This is probably the single biggest pitfall for bidders. Include cost estimating sheets for each major part of the project and describe the system used. Include labor charts, detailed data on direct and indirect labor costs, taxes, and travel. Estimate charges to overhead for everything from R&D to depreciation, logistics, training, documentation, and manuals. Bidders often wonder if government cost evaluators can possibly sift through the mountains of proposal cost estimates. You can bet that the major cost elements are put under a microscope. You'll be challenged during negotiations on the most trivial costs. But even if the evaluators pass over any of the thousands of cost elements in a bid, you can be sure that government auditors won't. Be prepared to defend what you bid—from the initial negotiations through contract performance and possibly through postcontract claims.

· Overlooking vital parts of the bid specification, drawing, or work statement. If you win the contract, the program office will force you to live up to every demand implied in the bid solicitation document, whether you priced such work in your proposal or not. The unexpected costs may come directly out of your pocket. RFPs for a federal office building included 106 different drawings—and one floor plan showed terrazzo stairways. The winning firm overlooked the terrazzo notation in the cost proposal and had to install the terrazzo stairs at $10,000 extra cost out of its profit.

· Failing to line up subcontractors or sources of supply before submitting the proposal. Don't assume you can go easily into the market to acquire material after you get the contract. If you run into any snags it's your tough luck, and you usually bear the cost of delays, higher prices, and possible damages to the government for your subcontractor failures.

Caution: Just because the IFB or RFP specifies a preferred source of supply or directed subcontractor, the prime contractor using such a sub is usually still responsible for the sub's performance. Unless Uncle Sam agrees to provide material physically as government-furnished equipment (GFE), the government does not guarantee the performance of any directed source of supply in a bid solicitation. One ammunition casing maker lost its shirt when a "preferred subcontractor" for copper flanges could not deliver because of copper shortages.

· Assuming that parts and components can be obtained for follow-on production bids for equipment long in Uncle Sam's inventory. Government agencies, particularly military services, often keep products in service long after they have become obsolete in the commercial market. Parts and components may no longer be manufactured by the original subcontractors—or anyone else, or the production volume on parts may have dropped to such a low level that it takes almost a custom-order price on any future order.

· As the prime contractor, relying on potential subcontractors to examine the IFB or RFP for technical and pricing help in preparing your bid. Such suppliers can misread or misinterpret bid specs. Primes may end up with a disastrous proposal if they fail to double-check each supplier opinion before inclusion. A building contractor relied on a plumbing supplier to price out kitchens for Army base housing, but the plumbing firm mistakenly felt the specs did not require dishwashers in 400 houses. The prime priced the proposal accordingly and later had to buy the 400 dishwashers with its own funds.

· Assuming that the government will furnish some material or service, when in reality the program office will claim that the IFB or RFP makes this the responsibility of the contractor. If you haven't priced such material or service in your proposal, you may well end up eating the extra costs. If in doubt about what Uncle Sam furnishes and what you furnish, ask during negotiating sessions. One RFP for overhauling Navy ships listed thousands of parts and subsystems with only a code letter distinguishing whether the Navy or contractor furnished the item. It was easy enough for the winning firm to confuse some of the code letters in preparing the cost proposal, but the winner ended up paying $93,432 for material that it had mistakenly assumed the Navy would provide.

· Failing to include special cost clauses to the contractor's advantage. Unless specifically prohibited by the RFP, special pricing terms, such as price escalation clauses to reflect inflation, prompt payment clauses, and the like, may only be added to a winning contract unless the bidder proposes them in the first place. Even when the RFP provides such special clauses, check carefully to be sure you are getting what you think you are proposing. One Air Force RFP had four major price sections; three included a price escalation clause, but the fourth section, the largest of all, did not include the inflation relief. An unwary bidder thought it was proposing a price inflation clause on all four sections but learned much later that the biggest cost part of the contract was not covered.

Strategy: The common pitfalls of cost proposals cover the mechanics of bidding, but the biggest pitfall of all, pricing strategies, requires a full chapter. (See Chapter 8, "Winning at Any Price.")

SO YOU MADE A MISTAKE

No one is perfect, least of all proposal writing teams laboring under pressure to meet deadlines. So mistakes can crop up in proposals— sometimes disastrous ones. During bidding negotiations, of course, a company can always amend its proposal to rectify an error, but after the final price deadline, any change could result in the proposal being thrown out. What about correcting a bid mistake after a firm has been selected to receive the contract or even been awarded the project?

Most procurement rules have a loophole that allows correction for honest clerical errors and inadvertent mistakes, particularly if no great change takes place. Friendly project officers may allow a favored vendor to take advantage of the loophole to stretch "clerical mistake" to allow questionable changes. One pet contractor did not bid a mandatory maintenance clause in the RFP. When irate losers protested, the firm quickly added the required maintenance agreement, with the friendly government contracting office agreeing the omission was a "clerical oversight."

It's more likely, however, that the agency will refuse to accept an alleged bidding mistake, especially from prols. After all, contract officials know they have a good deal—why voluntarily allow the contract price to go up? Sometimes a project office may ask a firm with an unusually low price to verify its offer, giving the company a chance to allege a bid mistake. Usually, however, if the company does claim a bid error, it cannot request a higher price but must either accept the contract at the original bid price or let the award go to the next lowest bidder. Often, agencies, smelling an unusually good deal, won't even seek to verify the low bid price. They just grab it and commit the unfortunate firm to honor its bid, mistake and all.

Usually proposals must be submitted by the bid due date deadline, but not always. It depends on how much vendors can get away with. Government contract offices have accepted late proposals for a variety of reasons. One agency allowed a bid to be delivered to the bid room twenty minutes late because of short staffing that day in the agency mail room. Other late bidders have convinced agencies that their proposals were delivered on time but mishandled by agency staffers. A telex bid response by one firm arrived fifteen minutes late but was allowed because Western Union testified to abnormally heavy traffic on the telex circuits. A few late bids have suspicious overtones—like the firm whose proposal arrived five minutes late and was exactly $1 less than the lowest price that had been bid up to that moment. (GAO allowed the late bid because the agency claimed that the bid had been misrouted by its own personnel, and GAO said it could find nothing improper in the bid's being $1 lower than the former low bid.)

> *Caution:* Some agency bid documents are so poorly written that they don't even list a time deadline on the day proposals are due. Without a specified cutoff time, however, contenders have little protection against late bids. Specifying "close of business" as the time bids are due is equally ambiguous and open to abuse for late bidding.

In the end, proposal writing is the key to getting almost all government business. The best technology, the greatest management skills are for naught unless a company can sell itself through its proposal. In most cases, no amount of marketing gamesmanship can make up for a badly written proposal. Learn the skill of proposal writing—you have no other choice.

8
WINNING AT ANY PRICE

- THE ULTIMATE LOW-PRICE BID: THE BUY-IN

- GETTING BAILED OUT WHEN YOU BID TOO LOW

- WHEN AGENCIES RUN A PRICE AUCTION ON A BID

- SEVEN PRICING STRATEGIES AND EIGHT PRICING PITFALLS TO AVOID

8. WINNING AT ANY PRICE

All too often, price is everything on government bids. The more agencies proclaim that they want to buy the best product or service regardless of price, the more they end up grabbing the lowest bid every time.

Of course, in an IFB or most two-step RFPs, the program office legally must award the contract to the low-price bidder, but these bids are a small factor in government procurement. Most acquisitions use negotiated RFPs, which are supposed to allow project offices to select the best possible winner, not an unqualified low-price bidder.

Even negotiated RFPs end up with bureaucrats tempted by low prices regardless of bidder qualifications. Picking the low price is an easy decision to defend, while justifying awarding the contract to the higher price bidder is more difficult, even if the proposal is judged superior. Often, program budgets are so tight that buyers jump at a cut-rate price that fits their strapped pocketbooks. Buyocrats frequently promote low prices by thinly disguised auctions during the bid cycle. In such price bludgeoning it is not surprising that they then grab the lowest price that they have wrung out of bidders.

Sometimes agencies deceive contenders or change desires in the middle of the bid. A program officer stresses, "We want the best technical proposal possible, not the cheapest. Put forth your best engineering effort." Watch out. At the last minute the officer may jump at the lowest price anyway or superiors in the agency may direct the program officer to take the low-price bid.

This puts bidders in a frightful dilemma. In some cases, an agency will stick to its guns and select the superior, higher price proposal. But contenders are caught in a vice: should they low-ball the bid price or make the all-out technical effort that comes with a higher price tag? A bidder's strategy must depend on the bidder's status (privileged, prime, or prol), how many contacts it has in the program office, how many accounting tricks it can get away with in the bid, how hungry it is for business, and what loopholes it can slip into the contract to rescue the firm if it wins.

The pressure is on vendors to bid a rock-bottom price—not just a low price, but a bare-bones low price, even a price that will lose money for the contractor. (GAO discretely points out that there is no law against bidding a below-profit price.)

BUY-IN AND BAIL-OUT

The ultimate low-price bid is the *buy-in*. A bidder simply guesses at the lowest price that competitors will propose and bids lower, regardless of the bidder's own cost estimates. To be doubly sure of winning, a buy-in bidder may shave off still another 5 to 10 percent. The goal is to win—at any price.

Buy-ins are a two-part strategy. To be successful, each buy-in must have a *bail-out*. That is the loophole, the back door, the safety valve that allows the buy-in bidder to recoup losses. It takes every bit as much skill to have a secret bail-out tied to your buy-in bid as it does to pull off a bridge finesse. For novices this strategy is akin to playing Russian roulette with the corporate assets. In a good game of "bid" the buyocrat knows you have a bail-out lurking somewhere behind your buy-in. The buyocrat wins by finding it and spoiling your escape; you win if the buyocrat spots it too late to stop it. In real life, project offices are often too lazy, too busy, or too desperate to keep a program going at any price, even on a bail-out; or, in some cases, they are too dumb to know they are being taken. All too frequently, a buy-in bidder doesn't have to conjure up a secret bail-out—the agency will do the job for the bidder. (See the section "Contract Changes" in Chapter 13.)

> *Watch:* Some contenders try to combine buy-in and bail-out in the same bid, which may not be allowed. If a firm cuts the price drastically on one part of the bid but jacks up the price in another part of the offer to offset the buy-in prices, the proposal is called "unbalanced" in procurement jargon. Unbalanced bids are strictly verboten. Even if the program office does not catch an unbalanced bid, eagle-eyed rivals most certainly will protest and may get your offer thrown out. Ideally, the agency spells out what type of pricing would be considered unbalanced, but this clause is frequently forgotten or is so ambiguous that bidders might risk some tricky pricing.

Most program offices chastise buy-ins. Yet the number that they snap up speaks louder than their oratory. Agencies have tried to draw up procurement rules to eliminate buy-ins, but the more regulations there are against the practice, the more it flourishes.

In their hearts buyers know that buy-ins just don't work. A company can't fulfill a contract well if it is losing money on the job; its bankers won't let it, even if the board of directors will. Unless the program office is willing to play bail-out, the stage is set for a major confrontation. The buy-in firm starts cutting corners, quibbling with program officials, asking for every manner of relief and extended delivery date.

Agencies are under strong pressure to give in. After all, if a project office was sucker enough to fall for a buy-in, officials don't want their foolishness exposed. Because there are so few checks and controls in government procurement, buyocrats have no great difficulty finding some pretext for the bail-out. The most common excuse is that the government changed contract specifications, so the contractor is due extra payment for the redesign. Of course, the extra funding covers more than the contract changes in order to rescue the firm from its original buy-in.

Other common bail-out excuses: the agency changes the program schedule, allowing extra costs for the delay; the original order is increased with enough added funding to offset the original buy-in; extra money is awarded for spare parts, training, or special technical manuals.

A simple bail-out is just accepting whatever the buy-in contractor can deliver. Original contract specs are downgraded for a variety of excuses (faulty government specs, urgent requirements dictate immediate delivery, original design too costly). The real reason, more often than not, is simply to cover up a buy-in. The government may end up in the worst of all possible bail-outs: being forced to raise contract funding sharply and still downgrade specs to attempt to get delivery on a lower quality product or service.

Another common bail-out is the usually legitimate price escalation clause. Ordinarily, these clauses protect both parties: the contractor on a fixed-price award is assured of some relief from runaway inflation and the agency has definite limits of liability. Unfortunately, these legitimate price escalation clauses are abused as bail-outs for contractors trying to recoup. Embarrassed buyocrats all too often go along with such ploys to hide their own mistakes.

Some friendly buyocrats don't even wait until the contract is signed before starting a bail-out. The Air Force selected one communications firm for final negotiations of a worldwide network and agreed to a final contract priced at $9 million, or 23 percent higher than the firm's original bid price.

A variation of bail-out is a "fake-out." A firm discovers after bid prices are revealed that in its feverish effort to win the award it bid far too low. Several ploys are used to get off the hook immediately:

· The low-price bidder finds a technicality in its bid as an excuse to claim a clerical mistake and seeks a higher price, although the price must still be less than that of the next lowest price bidder. Sometimes companies can get away with this strategy. *Caution:* Agency claims boards often refuse to consider alleged bidding mistakes if the project office does not allow them.

· Virtually all bids have a deadline, after which bidder prices expire. A firm can often count on government red tape holding up signing of the contract, and by throwing a little extra monkey wrench of some kind into the machinery, the firm can stall contract signing until after the bid price expires. This forces a new round of bidding, in which the firm hopes to raise its bid price but still remain below rivals. The ploy is good only when the company is assured that other contenders will not slash prices to try a buy-in on the second round of bidding.

Counterploy: Buy-ins are hard to fight if you are bidding honestly against one. GAO has held that a bidder can price its offer at a loss if it wants to. The RFP may have some clauses to protect against buy-ins, such as demanding full justification for any sharp reduction in price during the bid cycle. Contenders can cite such RFP prohibitions in protests to the agency and GAO in hopes of forcing a buy-in to be rejected. Sometimes appeals to higher officials in the agency may spur them to direct that a buy-in bid be rejected, especially if the agency has recently run into big trouble with a series of previous buy-ins.

BEST AND FINAL . . . AND FINAL . . . AND FINAL PRICES

Despite the agency party line against buy-ins, the government actually encourages and abets them by pressure-cooker bid tactics. Bureaucrats are possessed by a drive to get the best deal—in most cases this means the lowest price. Project officials score points for getting the price down to "save taxpayer money," and all too often this results in a situation that seems like extracting an extra pound of flesh from bidders.

Sometimes price leaks or innuendos dropped about competitive position in bids is enough to send rivals sharpening their pencils for new price cuts. A favorite technique is the "best-and-final price offer." Contenders submit their original prices and proposals, but after negotiations with program officials, they are given a new deadline to submit their best price offer. Theoretically, a best-and-final price offer allows a bidder to adjust its proposal in light of changes uncovered during negotiations. In practice, however, best-and-final price offerings end up as glorified auctions by the government.

Program offices may have two or even three best-and-final deadlines, driving prices lower with each round of supposedly final bidding. Turning the screws on price during a bid—especially during the critical final moments—too often just forces a buy-in by the bidder willing to lie the most.

Multiple best-and-final bidding rounds throw vendors into a quandary. Does an agency really mean "final," or will it have more rounds of best-and-final pricing? On the initial best-and-final deadline, a bidder may submit a price that is not as low as it intends to go, expecting to make bigger cuts on succeeding best-and-finals. However, the agency may have only one round, and the company is caught high and dry. Or the bidder may go initially with its truly final bid price, risking a leak to the other contenders in a prolonged bidding cycle. Rivals then undercut this price in succeeding rounds of bidding.

Higher authorities in government are aware of these abuses. A variety of schemes is being tried by many agencies to curb such price auctioning, but the techniques change rapidly, depending on the procurement fads of the moment. Suffice it to say here that most reform proposals fall into the same bureaucratic trap: the more regulations you add to cure a problem, the worse the problem gets. At this stage, best-and-final pricing or some variation appears firmly entrenched—although some reforms may come.

Many experts question the need for best-and-final deadlines at all. Any bidder on an RFP almost always had a chance to cut its price any time before the final contract award. Sometimes a desperate contender, unaware that it is already the low-price bidder, will whack back the price even further at the last minute before a contract winner is announced. A computer vendor, not knowing it was already 33 percent under the next nearest rival in price, cut another 5 percent off the bid the day before the winner was to be selected.

This brings up an exposed nerve in government procurement—leaking prices of various contenders during the bid cycle. Uncle Sam's procurement manuals never mention it. Agencies publicly deny that such leaks ever occur. As with most illegal practices, its extent is hard to judge. The truth probably lies somewhere between the bureaucrats' insistence that it never happens and industry's charges of rampant price exposures during bidding. When a contender wins a $10,000 contract by bidding $1 less than the next lowest bidder, one suspects a price leak. A $50 million electronic switch contract was won by a firm bidding only $3,000 less than the next lowest price contender. A coincidence or price leak?

Large companies—privileged and primes alike—employ an army of marketers to use everything from friendship, bribes, and eavesdropping to espionage tactics to ferret out any scrap of price information. A firm vying for a million-dollar Army truck order simply hired away a key engineer from a competitor, who came to work at the new job complete with intimate details of the rival's bid prices and technical proposal.

> *Counterploy:* To protect bid prices from leaks, use the "keep 'em guessing" strategy. Include a number of different options in a bid, each with its own price. During negotiations, ascertain which one the customer prefers, and only at the last minute make a final price offer on this option. Supposedly, the offer will be made too late for it to be leaked to rivals. Similarly, keep a special discount offer up your sleeve during most of the bid cycle. Spring it at the last minute when the impact may be greatest on the customer and when it is too late for leaks to competitors.

DESIGN TO PRICE: A NEW LINE ON PRICE

When developing a new product, an agency is as concerned with ultimate production price as it is with development cost. Uncle Sam has gotten stung far too often by contractors who bid a rock-bottom price to develop a new item, then stick it to the government when the product goes into production. Of course, the government can be just as guilty of running up costs of production, asking for all sorts of gingerbread and features that may not be essential but that shoot the price tag sky high.

Agencies use various tactics to hold down eventual production costs. Sometimes the production price is fixed in the original development contract—a so-called total package procurement. Now in disrepute, total package procurement is not dead; it appears in various guises such as quoting production options in the original development contract.

Another system used to control production prices is called "design to price." Contractors commit themselves to a target production unit price. Often project offices make it a sporty course by playing two contractors off against each other in competitive development, each contractor guaranteeing to meet a low design to price target production price tag. The goal is to design the item simply enough that its eventual production price will be kept low. But all too often, the system might as well be called "design to lie," as contractor and agency delude each other on the hoped-for final price.

Production may not come for many years, sometimes nearly a decade after development starts, so target production prices are continually adjusted upward to reflect yearly inflation rates. The government is always tinkering and making changes in a product under development; each change means that the target production price must be adjusted upward. The target production price, far from being a fixed commitment, is more like a moving target—hard to hit.

Any production price commitment can have a boomerang effect. Buyers will keep pumping money into the product's development phase, hoping to get a design that will hold to the original production price target. Savvy contractors have bailed themselves out of plenty of development squeezes with this ruse—and ended up getting higher production unit prices anyway, adjusted for inflation and government-ordered changes.

OTHER PRICING PRACTICES

Since price colors almost every other aspect of a bid, successful contractors keep a host of pricing tricks up their sleeves. Often the gimmick, the special twist, wins the award. Vendors soon learn that commercial pricing practices, figuring the cost of the job and tacking on an anticipated profit margin, just don't work on government bids.

Some systems used by successful bidders follow.

1. Bidding Slightly Under What the Agency Has Budgeted for the Job. Program budgets aren't too hard to ferret out. Often even the lowest engineer on the totem pole knows what has been allotted for the project. Other agencies obligingly publish budget data, especially in Congressional budget hearings. The budget bull's-eye pricing technique is widely used. On one military radio switch project, all bids came within $1000 of the $50 million budgeted amount.

> *Caution:* Agencies traditionally budget less than they realistically expect the program to run, with the hope that needed extra funding can be readily obtained once the program gets underway. But tagging a price proposal to such a low program budget may result in a loss to the contract winner, especially if the agency won't play bail-out.

2. Learning Whether Agency Has Made Independent Estimates of a Program's Cost, Regardless of the Amount Budgeted. Savvy vendors send feelers into agency offices before a bid comes out to ferret out such data. Often the agency asks an outside consulting firm to make the independent cost estimate. Vendors with friends inside the consulting firm can usually find out what this cost estimate is and bid accordingly.

3. Concealing a Normal, or Even Fat, Profit in a Package with Special Discounts and Out-Price Options. Such a bidder gambles that the project office will evaluate the bid on the basis of all the special discounts—which may never be exercised because of inept follow-through. For instance, firms often put in a high discount for payment within five or ten days, up to 10 or 12 percent. They may win the contract because the discount makes theirs the lowest price, but frequently the agency cannot process paperwork fast enough to make a short payment deadline.

> *Watch:* Some buyers try to claim the prompt payment discount even if Uncle Sam can't get the check to the contractor

by the required deadline, thinking a timid contractor won't want to make waves. An air base once refused any payment at all in a dispute over contract performance, and when it lost an ultimate claims fight, it still deducted the prompt payment discount—three years later. On another contract the Air Force took a prompt payment discount three months late, claiming the money was due the government anyway for faulty contract performance.

Watch: Some project offices fail to consider a bidder's prompt payment discount in evaluating its price. One firm lost a close bid that it should have won because the prompt payment discount was overlooked, while the selected winner gave none.

4. Using Tricky Options that Are Never Exercised to Score in Bid Evaluations. One firm offered a fantastic discount on leased equipment if the agency purchased $13 million in gear in precisely the fourteenth month of the contract—not one month before or after. The likelihood is slim that an agency can get such a large sum in the early stages of the contract and process paperwork in time to exercise the option.

5. Robbing Peter to Pay Paul to Work Out Low Price Proposals. One firm doesn't charge off corporate overhead expenses on this contract, but will sock it to other contracts to make up the difference. Another firm bids low to win initial production and makes it up in charges for spare parts, or special training, or documentation. One firm low-balls the price on one year's production of a highly proprietary Army aircraft navigation system—but jacks up the price on later years' orders because the Army is locked into the special navigation set.

6. Including a Price Escalation Clause in the Contract. Prols rarely can get one, but privileged firms and primes should insist on such terms, especially to protect themselves in times of rapid inflation. Although such clauses set a fixed percentage of escalation for any inflation impact, the trick is to load up the contract with extras—training, manuals, support costs, extra allowable expenses—to push up the base on which inflation escalation will be figured.

Prols are rarely offered these price escalation clauses, and most are too hungry to even ask for one. Even if they did, the agency would probably be quick to reject the demand. Perhaps a prol can cite precedent—finding a similar contract from the same agency that includes a price escalation clause—and shame the reluctant program office into giving equal treatment.

7. *Using a "Write-off."* Firms bid low, even at a loss, figuring the contract will put them into a new business line. Any new venture has high start-up costs, and it may be cheaper to write these off via a government contract. Losses can be charged off as nonrecurring development costs against future orders for the line Uncle Sam helped put you in.

Government bids are also full of unexpected pricing pitfalls. The largest primes often fall victim, and unwary prols are trapped by the thousands.

1. *Don't "Bet on the Come"—It Frequently Doesn't Come.* Agencies are masters at dangling the carrot of massive future orders before the eyes of hungry bidders. Inexperienced bidders—and even some veteran firms—low-ball their price for the initial contract, expecting to recoup with healthy future orders. But between bad planning and management, red tape, bureaucratic mind-changing, and many other procurement foul-ups, big follow-on orders are all too often cut drastically or never come at all. A Fortune 500 company dropped a bundle bidding on an initial laser development contract at a loss, counting on future orders for a handsome profit. But the project was canceled after two years, leaving a company that should have known better holding the bag.

2. *Agencies Frequently Ask for the Same Price on Limited Initial Orders and Large Follow-on Options.* The hooker is: the winning firm has no guarantee that the agency will ever exercise the follow-on options. A ship subsystems manufacturer bid a unit price of $10,020 on a huge order of 73,000 sets, projected over three years. However, after the first order of 195 units for sea tests, the Navy never went into production orders, leaving the firm swimming in red ink on its low price for so low a quantity.

Counterploy: Some contractors are demanding special clauses to get partial relief in case agencies drop programs after only limited initial orders. One firm got an agency to agree to buy back the unamortized cost of any special tooling and equipment that had to be ordered for the project when the long production run never came.

Counterploy: Keep the program agency approving subcontract orders for parts and components as far in advance as possible. Then if the project is dropped in midstream, the prime contractor has at least been paid for the parts, with profit tacked on. The prime may even get extra money as a claim for disposing of the surplus parts if the project is dropped. Even prols can play this strategy: one small Army contractor, suspecting a program cancellation, got an unwary project buyer to approve ordering an entire three years' supply of parts only months before the program was actually terminated.

3. *A Low Bid on Multiyear Leased Equipment Contracts or Long-Term Service Contracts Can Be Dangerous.* The contractor can be left high and dry if the contract is canceled midterm. A bus company quoted a low price for four-year transportation service on an Air Force base and even bought new buses to handle the contract. A base cutback after one year drastically cut the bus service, although the Air Force demanded the same cost per trip and refused to pay for the extra buses that were now idled.

Counterploy: Many firms seek stiff penalties if long-term lease or service contracts are curtailed or canceled before completion. Other companies give big discounts that are available only if the program runs the expected lifetime. Other firms will pass title of equipment to the government at the end of a long-term lease or give big bonus credits for converting the leased equipment to purchase if it is kept for the full expected lifetime.

Counterploy: Add special proprietary features and interfaces to installed equipment to make it costly for program offices to find similar products to replace your equipment. Develop unique software programs for data-processing gear, process-control systems, test equipment, machine tools, communications systems. It may become too costly for the user to replace the equipment if a new supplier must write entirely new software.

4. Never Assume Anything. Price every possible contingency. A contractor building Army barracks assumed the contract did not include storm windows on all units. It did, by inference. A service firm took over management of an officers' flying club and learned too late that it would have to have a qualified flight instructor on duty during all working hours, even though the club didn't have an instructor when the Army ran the facility. A sewer contractor expected Army buildings to be vacant when it had to rip up floors to lay new lines. Nothing was mentioned, and the contractor started to work, only to find out that it had to work around occupied buildings, costing an extra $800,000.

5. Don't Price on the Basis of Past Experience. Conditions change. Complacent established suppliers have turned in routine bids, only to find that sharp newcomers with lower overhead can beat the assumed price. There was the bidder who bought in on a contract, depending on long standing friendly relations with the contract office for a bail-out—only to find tough new contract officials refusing to grant any relief. Vendors on a high-priority missile project were accustomed to getting their asking price without question— when suddenly funds were cut and the low-priced vendors got the jobs.

Other assumptions can prove fatal. A small firm that had been shipping transmitters to the Army for years, one at a time, with the Army supplying the amplifier every time, rushed to meet an order for three transmitters and neglected to notice that this time the Army was *not* supplying the transmitters' amplifiers. The firm was thrown for a $17,205 loss.

Another firm had serviced Navy radios for years under a special Clause F, which was a blanket authorization for the firm to repair any defects and be reimbursed. One year Clause F was omitted from the contract, a fact the firm did not notice. Result: the company spent $23,700 on repairs that the Navy refused to pay for because there was suddenly no contractual obligation.

6. *Bid Your Price, Not Your Competitor's.* Too many contenders worry about what price rivals will bid and set their own strategy to beat that price. Firms that are positive they will be underbid by competition—and that cannot get the award on technical or other grounds—might be better off not bidding at all. Even government contractors must make a profit to stay in business; and unless a firm is confident of a bail-out, it would do well to bid a price that yields even a small return, regardless of what competition does.

7. *Be Sure You Can Live with Your Bid Price for a Long Time.* It may take six to eight months, even a year or more for the contract to be awarded. Most bid prices have an expiration date; otherwise, agencies could award contracts years later at the original bid price. Much the same thing happens anyway, as project offices ask contenders to keep extending bid prices during long delays. One Army bid for computer peripherals took so long that the low-price bidder had stopped production of the specific model by the time the Army was ready to make the contract award. The business went to a lucky runner-up at a much higher price. An Air Force bid for communications test equipment took so long that the low-price firm refused to extend its bid prices. Rather than go to a much higher priced runner-up, the Air Force canceled the bid and came out later with a new solicitation. The original low-price firm eventually ended up the winner on the second go-round but at a much higher price.

8. *Inflation Is a Fact of Life; Don't Ignore It.* Agencies love to tie up vendors with fixed-price, multiyear contracts. As inflation pushes prices up elsewhere, the project office ends up with a bigger bargain every year, to the dismay of the profit-squeezed supplier.

If the price escalation clause mentioned earlier is not in the contract, demand one. This will allow a certain percentage each year to cover inflation. A variation: quote follow-on quantities at a slightly higher price to cover expected inflation. Agencies are sticky about allowing any inflation relief. Many firms recoup by jacking up prices of spare parts or maintenance services. One firm, stuck in a multiyear, fixed-price bind, charged the Air Force 50 percent more to deliver extra quantities ordered under the contract. Even though this is contrary to economic theory, which says the larger the quantity, the lower the price, the vendor argued that larger orders necessitated expanded production lines with higher personnel training expenses—and the Air Force bought it.

Warning: If your own subcontractor's prices suddenly shoot up, don't count on Uncle Sam to pick up the extra tab on a fixed-price contract. Privileged firms can often force buyers to find some excuse for paying higher subcontract costs, but claims boards have been ruthless about holding other firms to original bids.

Caution: Adhere religiously to every small contractual detail on price escalation clauses. One firm notified the customer orally about an expected increase under the escalation clause but did not submit the proper government form requesting the increase until two months later. It was refused the increase for failure to give *written* thirty days' notice. Other companies may be refused price escalation for failing to submit all the required documents and supporting data.

Some firms with cost-reimbursal contracts misguidedly think that they are always covered on inflation. Often, however, an agency slaps a ceiling target cost on the contract; the supplier and the government may share any cost growth over this target or, in some cases, the firm may end up absorbing the whole overrun itself.

Vendors with fixed-price contracts often get hit with cost increases totally beyond their control. Claims boards have ruled that if Congress raises the minimum wage, a fixed-price contract cannot get any relief for being forced to assume higher wage costs.

The moral of all this is: plan the cost of your proposal carefully. You want to be a winner, not a loser, at any price.

9
NEGOTIATIONS—WHERE MOST SALES ARE REALLY MADE

- **WHAT NEGOTIATIONS COVER: PRICE, COSTS, PROFIT, TERMS AND CONDITIONS, TECHNICAL FINE POINTS**

- **WHO'S ON THE NEGOTIATING TEAMS FOR THE GOVERNMENT AND THE CONTRACTOR, AND THE PSYCHOLOGICAL WARFARE BETWEEN THEM**

- **COMMON GOVERNMENT NEGOTIATING PLOYS**

- **CONTRACTORS PLAY NEGOTIATING GAMES TOO**

9. NEGOTIATIONS—WHERE MOST SALES ARE REALLY MADE

The bid solicitation has gone out, proposals have been written, bids have been turned in. Now the real fun begins for RFP competitions. (IFB straight advertised bids are sporty, too, in a different way: everybody meets on the appointed day to open sealed bid envelopes and the low price automatically takes all.) RFPs are negotiated procurements—the low price may not win. Theoretically, an RFP allows the government to select the best possible product at the most reasonable price. At least, that's what it says in all the procurement manuals. Negotiations with all the bid contenders, based on their proposals, are supposed to accomplish this.

No two government bid negotiations are ever the same, just as no two commercial sales calls are ever the same. Even the same project office may conduct two widely varying negotiations on two different bids. The chemistry changes as the people change, both the government people and the other contractors; it varies according to time of fiscal year, whether the agency has just gotten budget clearance, or whether it risks losing appropriations that are not committed before the fiscal year ends. It shifts with the winds of political pressure, procurement techniques in vogue, and the past experiences of negotiators.

Veteran contractors approach each new negotiation from scratch. The unwary go into discussions with a canned strategy. ("It worked last time so it ought to be good enough for these negotiations.") The smart contender sizes up each bid, the project office and the personalities involved, the best information on budget funds, how urgently the contract is needed—and plots negotiating strategy accordingly.

The first surprise facing even long-established firms is that they may prepare thoroughly for negotiations and never be called in. There is nothing in the procurement regulations to force agencies to negotiate with all contenders. GAO has ruled that agencies should negotiate with all qualified bidders with prices "in a competitive range" (a range that is ambiguous and open to endless debate), but even this GAO finding has enough loopholes to allow any buying office to simply ignore negotiations altogether and award a contract on the basis of proposals and prices submitted.

Disheartened bidders can scream that they were never given a chance to explain their complicated proposals. They may even suspect a disguised sole-source award to a favored vendor, with the project office merely going through the charade of an RFP to meet the letter, if not the spirit, of procurement regulations. But it won't do them any good.

Happily or unhappily, depending on the course of the negotiations, most RFP bids go into face-to-face discussions between buyers and contractor officials. Here the two sides will be sure they understand precisely what is involved: agencies ensure that they understand all parts of the company proposal, and bidders make sure that they comprehend exactly what the government wants. This is supposed to remove all misunderstandings and faulty interpretations, since few RFPs are ever written so explicitly that they answer everyone's questions. Negotiations also give firms a chance to get a feel for the project.

Caution: If the project office is confused on the requirements or has a battle inside the agency defending the project, knowledgeable firms adapt their bidding strategy to protect themselves in case they win such a confused contract because it is destined for trouble. Such a project is a great candidate for future contract changes (all at an extra high price, of course) as the project office tries to correct its own earlier mistakes. (See "Contract Changes" in Chapter 13.)

Warning: A great danger is the leaking of a vendor's technical approach to other contenders during negotiations. Buyers can either do this deliberately ("Let's combine the best of everyone's proposals") or inadvertently simply by asking about alternative approaches. This transfusion of technical ideas during negotiations is hardly fair to bidders that make exhaustive efforts to prepare a truly innovative bid. But since federal bids aren't copyrighted, ingenious bidders may find their best ideas stolen from them during negotiations, with a competitor winning the contract to put the concept into effect. A large space satellite builder protested unsuccessfully to GAO that its unique spacecraft design was transferred during NASA negotiations to a competitor, which won the $100 million award to build it.

Industry complaints have grown so loud that a mass of new agency procurement directives and new bidding techniques have been added to the staggering library of rules to curb this problem. At this point there is still no guarantee that buyers can be prevented from deviously prompting negotiating bidders toward a desired technical approach.

One common method of transferring technical concepts comes from agencies' pointing out deficiencies of a firm's proposal during negotiations. In fact, GAO has overturned some bids because government negotiators didn't point out a firm's proposal deficiencies. (In typical federal doublethink, GAO has rejected other protests that claimed that federal negotiations failed to point out bid deficiencies—so you pay your money and take your choice on this issue.) Theoretically, a project office points out a bidder's deficiencies so the firm can correct them for any eventual contract that may be signed, but if an agency points out one firm's shortcomings, it must do the same for all contenders. In practice, agencies frequently point out supposed deficiencies that don't correspond to their own preconceived notions. Sometimes agencies put a favored vendor into contention by pointing out all its bid deficiencies, after having been alerted to such shortcomings by the superior technical proposals of rivals.

Some areas that negotiating sessions usually cover follow.

Price. At the very least, both sides must be sure they completely understand all costs involved in a firm's bid. (See Chapter 8, "Winning at Any Price.") The government is likely to demand exhaustive documentation to support every major cost element. Negotiators may haggle over rates for labor, overhead charges, nonrecurring costs, and material costs. Firms trying to buy in to a contract are supposed to be challenged to support such low prices or risk being thrown out of the bid. In reality, buyers who want buy-ins to show all the taxpayer money that they are saving will probably challenge realistic prices to drive these prices down. Know your project office before you go in—that's how the veterans protect themselves.

All the terms and conditions of the contract, including hundreds of boilerplate clauses, are subject to negotiation. Buyers will press hard to get bidders to agree to clauses most favorable to the government, but scores of terms and conditions may never come up at all. Be prepared to bring up objectionable terms yourself. You must also ask about any ambiguous or boilerplate clauses now. After the contract is signed, it is too late. Many a careless firm has discovered to its horror that an overlooked clause buried in the hundred pages of the pact will cost the company tens of thousands of dollars. A housing contractor found that a contract to make military apartments ready for occupancy included a telephone installation clause—$15 per apartment, resulting in an extra cost of $4500 out of the contractor's own funds. In another case, the revamping of a large air base called for "relocating radar equipment." The contractor assumed that the Air Force would handle this, but the project office said the Air Force would only provide trucks to move the big equipment. The company bore the rest of the cost—a mistake it might have avoided if details had been brought up during negotiations.

A contractor negotiates with a battery of government officials, many of them coming and going throughout the discussions. New government specialists may come into the sessions late in the game. If agencies fear that negotiations are not going well, higher level officials may be called in. The shifting cast of government people as well as the sheer number of them make consistent personal discussions difficult. The contractor may never know who's really the leader of the government team and who are the main individuals to persuade to accept the firm's position.

Often, contractors are so awed by the legal trappings that they do not recognize the human element. Negotiators on both sides are people, bringing all their foibles, biases, and past experiences to the bargaining table. A bidder with a perfectly acceptable proposal can lose the contract by rubbing key government officials the wrong way. One contractor was heading toward an obvious contract signing, when negotiations broke down because of a bitter dispute over fine technical points between the government and company engineers.

Negotiations often resemble psychology lab exercises, as each side tries to out-psyche the other. Some agencies make sure their negotiators are trained in psychological principles, besides possessing the necessary legal background. (So do some companies.) However, competent bidders need not fear being brainwashed in stage-managed negotiations. A firm should know its objectives before coming to the table—and stick to its strategy. Engaging in psychological warfare with the Feds can be entertaining, but it can also sidetrack any meaningful discussion.

Where should negotiations be held? Some companies try to force government negotiators to come to their plant—or at least their city—figuring this gives the firm a home-court advantage. It also allows company negotiators to send out quickly for any needed data or to call in any technical or legal experts. However, the advantage can be offset by constant distractions, as key company officials are called away from negotiating sessions for office problems. Sending a negotiating team to the agency's locale is more expensive, but it can also have added benefits. The company negotiators are together constantly throughout the discussions and can develop real teamwork.

Wherever negotiations are held, be sure key company experts on all parts of the proposal—legal, technical, administrative—are present throughout the discussions. Don't send technical specialists home when negotiations come to the point of discussing profit because you feel this is not their area. Profit issues may have a high technical factor, and you'll need all the expert help you can get.

Some contractors like to form a professional team that handles all negotiations for every bid. Small firms with limited personnel resources have no other choice. Such a constant team can have great expertise and develop finely tuned negotiating skills. A drawback may be lack of flexibility and missing key inputs from specialists not on the team. Also, the team leader is tempted to become a dictator, often tearing apart a negotiating team.

To be successful, bidders should be aware of commonly used negotiating ploys. Some strategies on the government side follow.

1. Don't Tell Them Anything. Force the bidder to play Sherlock Holmes to pry out the project office's real intentions, or to discover where the real payoff is in the program.

> Counterploy: Two can play the same game, even prols. Don't lay down your hand until the bureaucrats show their cards; or deliberately misinterpret government's position, forcing federal negotiators to correct the misunderstanding, exposing their true goals.

2. Tell Them Everything. Bury discussions in an avalanche of details, trivia, documents—thus diverting attention from controversial boilerplate clauses buried deep in the proposal. Overkill can keep bidders guessing about the real intentions of government negotiations just as well as telling them nothing.

3. Turn Everybody On–Make Each Bidder Think It Is a Sure Winner. Get the bidder to cut the price an extra 10 percent or accept certain contract demands.

> *Counterploy:* Get good inside intelligence to find out if negotiators are putting you on. Also play "let's see the color of your money." Use a counter-hooker—put a string on the bait ("I'll give you what you want but only on my terms").

4. Stall for Time. Bureaucrats don't have approved funds yet, but they go through the entire process as if they did. Negotiations can be strung out for months until the agency finally gets its money. Another variation: two rival agencies are competing for similar programs, but probably only one will go ahead.

> *Counterploy:* Inside intelligence. Also, play the false front game: during a long negotiation stretchout, assign key talent to other, more productive projects, but keep the appearance of a negotiating team that is as strong as ever.

5. Go for the Jugular. The agency's objective is to find the weakness of each bidder—and twist it to the government's advantage. Is the firm desperate for business? Then the agency makes the firm think that competitors are right on its heels. Has the bidder given a big discount on another agency contract? Then the agency demands the same—or more. Has a bidder mistakenly overestimated costs on some parts of its proposal? Then the agency all but brings down the wrath of God to get the bidder to lower this cost estimate—as well as the prices on all other parts of the proposal.

> *Counterploy:* Go for the buyer's jugular. Does the agency have an urgent immediate need? Then stress in negotiations early assured delivery and performance. Is political pressure mounting? Then point out that a fast award (to you, of course) will get the project underway.

Strategies that bidders can use follow.

1. Tell Them Everything They Want to Believe. Project officials don't want to be told they are taking the wrong approach. Smart bidders don't throw out pet brainstorms. They learn what the buyocracy really wants and promise it—even if the bidder knows it won't work. Bail-out is almost assured for these contract winners, since bureaucratic necks are on the block to make the pet ideas work out.

2. Play the Corporate Versions of Sherlock Holmes. This is difficult, since government negotiators have an arsenal of laws to demand detailed data on bidder prices, costs, accounting systems, sources of supply, credit and financing. However, if firms don't tip their hands early, they may discover government strategy simply from the questions negotiators ask in trying to draw you out.

Caution: Don't be so secretive that your position never gets on the table. The negotiations may suddenly end before you have fully explained your case.

3. Find the Hidden Trick. Many times, you can't tell just by the way the RFP is written if it is rigged for a favored vendor. But you may uncover a bias during negotiations—especially if it appears that specifications, technical approaches, terms, and conditions are slanted to a competitor. The sooner you uncover such information, the greater are your chances of mounting a successful challenge.

4. Fill in the Missing Pieces. If the RFP is fuzzy, if specs are hazy, drawings incomplete, this is the time to force buying offices to fill in the blanks, unless you intend to play "bail-out because it's your fault the bid package was lousy." If government negotiators can't come up with firm answers, be sure to put enough waivers in the contract to protect yourself against future problems, which are sure to arise.

5. Use the Sudden Carrot. Drop a juicy discount, option, or giveaway at the right moment during negotiations. If the timing is right, this may even steal a rigged bid away from the favored vendor.

Caution: Don't give away more than you can afford unless you are certain of a bail-out. Ingenious bidders can come up with special terms that look like the government is making a killing but that don't cost the company that much. One Fortune 500 company leased equipment at full list price—but offered extra rental credit if the government converted to purchase. The credits looked better than they were because they were based on a high rental price to start with.

6. *Keep'em Guessing on Price.* Be sure you have a chance to adjust your price downward before the end of negotiations; then start negotiating with a fictitious higher price. This protects against price leaks to the competition during negotiations—and may even mislead rivals if your original inflated price is exposed.

7. *Snoop Out the Competition.* The answers of government negotiators to technical questions or pricing strategies can tip you off to what they have heard from other vendors. Watch especially for signs that the bid is wired in for a favored vendor. Be cautious about volunteered leaks from agency negotiators—they could be misleading you about where the competition stands.

8. *Play Cross-Examination to Double-check Government Claims.* Phrase questions several different ways at various times during discussions and to different government people. Be sure all the answers are consistent—or find out why the responses differ. State the government position in slightly different ways, and check reactions of all government representatives.

In addition to various strategies that both sides use during negotiations, there are some common-sense rules for all parties to achieve meaningful discussions:

1. *Each Side Must Be Certain It Understands Precisely What the Other Wants.* This is not always easy, considering the number of people and the hundreds of technical, pricing, cost, and contractual terms involved. Serious misunderstandings by either party can lead to major contract snags. A construction firm replacing six huge interim aviation fuel storage tanks at an air base bid a bargain price, mistakenly assuming it would acquire the existing temporary tanks being dismantled. It didn't. Had the firm clarified the question during negotiations, it could have adjusted its price rather than taking an unexpected loss on the work. The time to iron out misinterpretations is at the negotiating table—not in protracted court fights years later.

2. Neither Side Should Be So Locked in to Its Position that It Cannot Bend. Too often, buyocrats play the heavy hand, insisting on predetermined contract terms. This is partly because of layered bureaucracy. Agency superiors have given negotiators a target position even before talks begin, and underlings are afraid to deviate in any way. Many times, an agency can break down one of the bidders to agree to the most onerous of contract conditions—but this may be the weakest contender, the one least able to resist government pressure. Winning the negotiating battle but losing the ultimate contract performance is poor policy. Do your firm and your country a service. Refuse to get backed into such a corner. Complain when it happens.

3. Put It in Writing. Verbal agreements may not end up in the final contract. Oral interpretations of complex terms and conditions provide no record if there are contract disputes. Written agreements prevent misunderstandings and prevent the other side from claiming a different interpretation later.

> *Caution:* There is a right time for reaching written agreements. Too legalistic an approach too early in discussions may backfire. Preliminary written statements tend to seal positions in concrete too soon, making concessions or change difficult.

4. Negotiations Are Not the Place to Start a Completely New Bid. Agencies may try to significantly change the terms and requirements beyond the RFP. Companies should resist any attempt to turn negotiations into an entirely new bid. Demands not in the original RFP are not mandatory. If a bidder puts new conditions that buyers like on the negotiating table, they must amend the RFP to give other contenders a chance to respond to the same conditions.

Suppose a bidder finds itself in the enviable position of being the only firm to respond to a government solicitation. Agencies often go to great lengths to conceal this fact, but it is not hard for an alert firm to find out that it may be in the driver's seat during negotiations. Most knowledgeable firms know who their competition is, and cocktail party talk, industry gossip, and just querying rivals can give a good idea who did not bid. Even sources within the agency can tip off the lucky sole bidder.

Unhappily, this can be the most difficult negotiation of all. Since agencies cannot award the contract to someone else, negotiators must now resort to every trick in their bargaining bag to cajole, fake, or threaten the single bidder to try to get a reduced price or better terms. Buyers do have effective clout even here: if a sole bidder remains too obstinate, the agency can cancel the bid altogether for a variety of reasons (insufficient competition, changing requirements, lack of faith in negotiations). After cancellation, the agency may go sole-source to meet what is now certainly an urgent requirement. A stevedore firm—the only bidder in a particular situation—held fast to its price, only to find the Navy military traffic command canceling the bid and acquiring the service sole-source under a basic order agreement signed earlier with a rival firm.

Everything said about single-bid negotiations also applies to sole-source contracts. Unless the agency is totally committed to giving a privileged or favored prime almost everything demanded, government negotiators may put up a stiff front even negotiating a sole-source pact.

Counterploy: This is a good time for firms on the outside to try to head off sole-source awards. A shrewd computer memory manufacturer literally stole a pending sole-source award away from its rival while negotiations dragged on; the outsider submitted an unsolicited proposal at prices far below the proposed sole-source rates.

No broad guidebook can possibly cover such an intricate legal interplay as negotiations. Universities, management associations, consultants, and industry groups run frequent short courses, seminars, and training sessions on negotiations. Some are very good— others, pretty bad. Evaluate any presentation by the colors it bears. If it promises to hand out only the buyocracy party line, you may end up wasting your time. Only briefings that give the real-world view of negotiations, from legal sleight-of-hand to psychological gamesmanship, will be of any use.

In the long run, contractors become knowledgeable negotiators just by negotiating. The nuances, skills, and human element cannot be reduced to textbook formulas. And, since every negotiation is different, even veteran industry contract officials are constantly learning. Keeping pace with the changing nature of negotiations is part of the sport. May the best team win.

10
PROFIT IS NOT A DIRTY WORD

10. PROFIT IS NOT A DIRTY WORD

On many government contracts the bottom line is a battle line between vendors and buyocrats.

Companies obviously need a reasonable profit return. Many times, vendors must get more than an average profit to compensate for the high cost of selling to Uncle Sam. In a few cases, privileged vendors and a few primes are out to get what the market will bear.

When buying offices are giving one vendor favored status or are sole-sourcing the award, government contract officials often willingly accede to the contractor's expected profit return unless it is completely out of line. Actually, there are so many ways to camouflage profits on complex government contracts that agencies dealing with favored suppliers need not fear reprimands if they play their cards carefully.

If agencies have no preordained favorites, it can be open season on negotiated profits for the winning firm. Contract officials score their marks by how low a price they can get. Negotiators are often schooled in countless ways to force contractors to agree to lower profit. Vendors often suspect that government negotiators may get higher proficiency ratings in their personnel records for carving out an extra pound of flesh from bidders in a bitter competition. Agencies vigorously deny this, but even so, in wide-open bids, subtle pressure is on government negotiators to bargain for extremely close contractor profit.

This is a far cry from the commercial market. In dealing with each other, companies may negotiate vigorously, but each party generally recognizes the need for the other to earn a reasonable return.

Buyocrats' antipathy to contractor profit also runs counter to the government's own best interests. Few factors motivate businesspeople more than profit. Economic logic says: if you want to get the greatest contractor effort on a project, you maximize the opportunity for profit.

Even the bureaucracy party line often concedes that the government could stimulate contractors to greater performance through greater profit incentives. Government procurement conferences, directives, pronouncements, and speeches are replete with good words on using profits to motivate vendors.

But profits, like many other factors in the jumbled world of federal procurement, are a paradox. No matter what project offices claim publicly, they are influenced by these subconscious realities:

- Government negotiators only get credit for tough contracts. It may be years before the fruits of the contract—a new product or service—are delivered, and someone else will get credit if the end result is good. There's little percentage in using profits to get better contractor performance if someone else gets all the glory.

- On the other hand, government auditors can criticize liberal contract profits, and that could end up a minus in the negotiator's personnel file. The General Accounting Office, Congress members on a tirade, or opponents within the same agency often attack "giveaways" and "windfall profits." The safest course is the tight fist.

- Even if bureaus negotiate profit incentives in one part of the contract, they can take away earnings in another part of the pact. Janus negotiators often agree to a higher profit return, only to impose stringent conditions or force contractors to assume greater liabilities, which eat up any extra earnings. A power generator firm was given an Army award with a sliding scale incentive equal to 20 percent extra payment if the firm met tight delivery dates and high performance specs. But the pact spelled out so many stringent tests and exhaustive reports that the firm ended up with an extra incentive payment of $3.49.

- Some officials assume that contractors don't deserve any more profits than they get because Uncle Sam provides them with so much help. Government assistance on contracts can be substantial. Firms can get twice-monthly progress payments on government pacts, greatly reducing their need to borrow funds. Uncle Sam can furnish tooling, test equipment, material subsystems—even provide the factory where the product is built. While all this may be true, federal contractors must still foot what is often a substantial bill themselves. Such a "Big Daddy" tight fist can be counterproductive. Contractors may have less and less incentive to invest in government work, living instead off government contract doles. Company management will invest more of the firm's own capital on contract work only if there is greater reward.

The profit negotiating battle often dooms contracts right from the start. Hard-nosed government negotiators wring the last ounce of profit out of a contract before it is signed. This sets up vendor and agency as adversaries on all future contract work: the supplier works all angles to recoup some of the profit it was forced to give up in order to get the award in the first place, and buyocrats struggle to plug all loopholes for any more profit. All too often, each side becomes more concerned with this cat-and-mouse fencing than with getting a good product or service.

A particular profit straitjacket is the cost-sharing contract. Agency offices find they have so many hungry bidders that they can force the winning firm to absorb a large share of the contract cost, with the contractor's payoff coming later on promised big production orders. Traditional cost sharing is fifty-fifty between the government and the contractor, but sometimes vendors are forced to absorb as much as 66 percent of the cost. The Army was negotiating for the development of a new artillery-fire control computer and hadn't thought of cost sharing until a desperate bidder offered to split the development costs fifty-fifty. Army negotiators thought that was a good idea—but instead of accepting the initial firm's offer, Army bargainers played "can you top this" to get an even hungrier bidder to share 60 percent of the cost.

> *Caution:* Uncle Sam should pay his full share of the costs of any product or service being used exclusively by the government. Forcing vendors to bankroll a project only sets up a future showdown between the agency and the company as it tries to recoup its investment. Cost sharing is legitimate only when the contractor will end up with a potential commercial product out of the government-funded project. In that case, Uncle is correct in making the company pick up part of the tab. On some unfortunate fixed-price contracts, vendors may end up cost sharing unwillingly if program expenses exceed the ceiling price.

Most negotiating battles center around the allowable profit rate on a contract. Such a rate can be expressed in an almost infinite number of formulas, percentages, ratios, or fixed sums. Some government profit formulas look like Einsteinian equations. Much sound and fury during negotiations can occur over a fraction of a percentage point profit on any of a myriad of contract elements. This turmoil often blinds both parties to the economic fact that profit is made up of many elements.

To come out ahead, a company must remember that:

Final Return = Negotiated profit − Unallowable costs
+ Fringe payments

Of these, unallowed costs, which the contractor must pay out of its own funds, affect contract return as much as the negotiated profit rate itself.

There are basic costs that the government traditionally has not allowed to be charged off against contracts: most advertising, interest on borrowed working capital, entertainment, contributions.

In addition, agencies place varying restrictions on charging off other costs: depreciation, interest on loans for new plant and equipment, travel, home office expenses, allocations of research and development, proposal costs. Beyond these basic costs, parts of almost every single cost element of the contract, from labor rates to material costs to general administrative overhead, may not be allowed. Every dollar that the contractor must then spend out of its own funds reduces the earnings return of the contract—no matter what profit rate the contractor may have negotiated.

Conversely, fringe payments can increase contractor return above the negotiated profit rate. Most common fringe payments are various types of fees awarded for surpassing specified contract goals and objectives. There are almost as many different incentives as profit rate formulas, and the target thresholds for qualifying for such rewards can be equally varied. Incentives can be a two-edged sword: they may come with corresponding penalties if the contractor fails to meet minimum contract targets. Just to complicate the contract further, baseline target objectives spelled out in the original contract may be constantly adjusted to reflect inflation, engineering changes, altered scope of work, or new contract requirements.

Neophytes soon learn that negotiating an incentive fee into a contract is one thing; getting the government to pay what the company believes is its due is quite another. Profit battles may merely shift from the negotiating table to the squabble over whether or not the firm met contractual incentive goals. An unlucky firm may end up spending all its contract profit on legal fees fighting claims to get the incentive payments.

There are other less obvious fringe payments. Privileged firms and primes often can get extra funding from agencies for independent research and development (IR&D). The Department of Defense and some large civilian agencies have long recognized that contractors invest some of their own funds in basic or exploratory research that may open up unexpected technical breakthroughs or innovations. These agencies will then negotiate a small extra percentage of the firm's total annual contracts to be awarded for the IR&D. The theory is that the government benefits from and wants to encourage innovative research over and above the very detailed and structured federal contract.

IR&D can be an especially valuable extra to a firm. It allows a creative staff to come up with novel concepts that can become unsolicited proposals or can be used to presell agencies and wire in future competitive bids. Generally, only bigger firms get IR&D funding. However, the qualification rules are ambiguous, and it is worth the try for any contractor, no matter what size, to demand IR&D funding if it can make a case for extra research work.

Another hidden profit bonus is to let Uncle Sam pick up the tab for most nonrecurring costs on a major new product. If the product being built for the government can be adapted for the commercial market, a firm is already ahead of competitors that must fund nonrecurring development and start-up costs out of their own pockets. Many firms are willing to take a razor-slim profit on a federal contract—or perhaps even a loss—to get such nonrecurring cost assists. Even if the product has little or no commercial value, a firm may get a big boost on nonrecurring costs for bidding the same or similar product for other government contracts.

Caution: The nonrecurring cost write-off can work in reverse: a largely commercial firm that gets a big government contract may end up having to charge off start-up costs to its commercial operations overhead because of very low government contract earnings. Industry increasingly challenges the myth that Uncle Sam is footing the commercial market costs of government contractors. Too often it is just the other way around, they charge. Only astute negotiating by companies can force Uncle to pay his full share of costs—government negotiators get their kudos from every cost element they force contractors to absorb.

Profits for government work vary enormously from contract to contract, from agency to agency, and even within the same program office. However, a few guidelines that hold true for major contract types follow.

Invitation for Bid (IFB). Profits on this fixed-price, one-shot procurement in which the lowest bid is always the winner are really nobody's business but the bidder's. Competition is supposed to assure that the winner cannot gouge Uncle Sam too badly. In fact, competition is generally so severe on IFBs that bidders often end up gouging themselves. Straight advertised bids tend to return very low profit—the rock-bottom price needed to win forces very slim returns.

> *Counterploy:* Even fiercely bid IFB procurements have loopholes for increasing profits. Spare parts, training, documentation, follow-on orders, service support, engineering change proposals (ECP)—all can be priced at far higher profit. A smart agency will force bidders to price as many of these extras as possible in the original contract, thus closing off these profit escape routes. But if there's no contract price for any extra customer needs, vendors can try to recoup on earnings. After all, even the lowliest prol may now find itself a sole source for selling these extra services—and can price accordingly.

RFP for Fixed-Price Contract. Here also, competition is supposed to hold down bid prices—and hence, the winning contractor's profit. But, unlike IFBs, the negotiated fixed-price contract from an RFP puts buyers much more into the vendor's business. Even though the contractor agrees to live within the ceiling of its fixed-price bid—including the profit return—the actual profit rate is negotiated. That subjects bidders to the microscopic review of costs, facilities, management, and accounting systems which, we have seen, is the very fabric of contract negotiations. Adjustment of any of these factors in the final contract can have a great impact on the firm's expected profit, sending it either up or down. The exact profit rate on the contract, even though the price is fixed, is also subject to intense negotiation. If project officials can drive down the negotiated profit, the contractor may be forced to accept a lower contract price than it originally bid.

RFP for Cost Reimbursal Contract. Bargaining is toughest for cost-plus awards, since federal negotiators see a potential profit boogeyman behind every cost estimate in the vendor's original bid. Uncle Sam ends up paying all the costs, no matter how high, unless some type of cost sharing or cost growth ceiling is negotiated. The higher the cost, the more profit a contractor can earn, unless the contract is tightly monitored and controlled.

For this reason, scrutiny is intense on almost every element of the bidder's estimated costs. Detailed documentation to justify even the lowest component level and most minute labor job is usually needed. Misguided vendors often think they can play sleight-of-hand accounting to hide real costs, but even if trick cost estimating slips by the original contract negotiators, be assured that government auditors will probably uncover the accounting charade later. If they miss it, the Renegotiation Board can charge that the firm made excess profits and demand partial refund. (See Chapter 15, "Audits—You Oughta Done Differently.")

Contract offices, fearful that cost-plus contracts with no strings attached may leave the government vulnerable to runaway costs, may try to negotiate a target ceiling. A firm would then be forced to absorb all costs above this expense lid. Or buyers may agree to share the overrun costs on some type of split formula. In either case, the firm's profit can be affected disastrously in case of a large overrun. Even if a firm didn't buy-in on such a cost-ceiling contract, it better be sure there are bail-outs to protect it in case the ceiling is surpassed.

Incentive Fee. Agencies have found that the layers of restrictions, excessive paperwork, and low bid profit margins on ordinary contracts often turn vendors off instead of stimulating them to do their best work. To put a carrot back into the contract, the incentive fee has been developed. If a vendor meets certain specified milestones or benchmark tests, the firm qualifies for bonus payments. The contractor may get incentive payments for meeting cost targets, beating delivery schedules, or achieving higher reliability goals. Often, negotiations over incentive fees can be as vigorous as over the main contract itself—for the vendor knows that this is an area in which it can pick up extra profit, often turning a marginally successful contract into a real winner. Agency project offices, on the other hand, often fight hard against any large incentive bonuses, fearing they may be criticized later if a vendor ends up with large bonus profits, even for delivering a better product.

Sometimes the incentive clause is coupled with penalties for failing to meet specified performance or cost levels. Prols and some primes should be wary—they could lose their shirts for missing targets for a variety of unexpected reasons. Not only can favored vendors frequently avoid penalties; their real coup is getting incentive payments even on troubled projects. One satellite builder got a $4 million bonus payment when its project was three years late and the cost had tripled. This reverse whammy is achieved by claiming that all delays and increased costs are the result of government-ordered changes. Thus, technically, the firm is still meeting its target—since all changes are Uncle Sam's fault.

Disallowed Costs. As we have seen, agencies will try to restrict a wide range of costs in the contract, and every disallowed cost can eat heavily into the profit. Often, cost elements are not barred entirely, but only a small percentage is allowed. Thus, only a small portion of a firm's general administrative overhead may be written off on a specific contract; or labor rates in the contract are, in effect, lower than actual labor costs because fringe benefits or some portion of overtime costs are not allowed; or contributions to pension plans, employee stock plans, and worker thrift plans can be disputed and not fully reimbursed by the government. Depreciation of equipment, plant investment, and the cost capital borrowing are bones of contention not always fully chargeable to government contracts.

The profit problem snarls contractors because no two agencies have the same profit policy. Many agencies differ even from one contracting office to another.

This keeps an army of accountants, lawyers, and contract specialists employed in the big firms. Since Uncle Sam ultimately ends up paying the price for these massive extra staffs, either directly as contract costs or through higher prices, many observers have campaigned for uniform governmentwide profit directives. These savants point out that the commercial market does not force companies to engage thousands of extra specialists to cope with a bewildering array of conflicting and confusing profit policies. However, there is no one government market, but literally thousands of markets—as many as there are contract offices seeking bids. Moreover, any efforts by the White House or superagency authorities to mandate uniform profit policies runs into Finagle's Fourth Law: "The more that is done to correct a situation, the worse the problem gets"; or "Every directive creates its own loopholes."

The small contractor has little hope of employing enough specialists to cope with the welter of profit policies and many times unexpectedly finds itself on the short end of a contract because it didn't prepare for the pitfalls ahead.

Strategy: Just as in commercial marketing, small businesses do better if they sell a few customers (in this case, contract offices) that they know well so they will be better able to defend their contract positions. They can learn the profit policies of the few customers they pick out. In a few cases, they may be better informed than their giant competitors who are covering all the federal waterfront. One caution: just because a long-time agency customer has treated profit issues the same way for years does not mean it won't unexpectedly shift to new contracting gimmicks that could heavily impair profits.

On the positive side, the confusing welter of policies creates situations in which adept industry negotiators can score mightily. One savvy contractor made sure it got incentive fees no matter how many engineering changes the government signed on the project. Thus, the worse the agency managed the project, forcing more and more changes, the more incentive payments the firm received for every contract price increase.

One might wonder why companies continue to put up with these problems and even vie vigorously for the business. The reasons:

· The contract profit picture can have a rosier side. The earnings return, as a percentage of the contract price, may be lower than comparable profit margins in the commercial market, but profits, as a percentage of capital invested, tend to be much higher in government business. We've mentioned government-furnished tooling, production equipment, materials, engineering drawings, software, even federal employees to work on the project, and the possibility of twice-monthly progress payments during the life of the contract cutting down the amount of working capital that must be borrowed.

As we have warned, project offices may use this government assistance as an argument to cut down company profits on other legitimate contractor-borne investment. But if a firm can protect its legitimate profits, it can usually expect a greater return on capital investment than it will get in the commercial market.

· Many contracts fluctuate so widely, have so many different cost elements, and cover such a long period, it is often nearly impossible for even the largest firm to know precisely the profit earned until years after the project is completed. The illusion of profit may exist even when the ultimate outcome is a loss. When a company has dozens to hundreds of government contracts going at any one time, all in different states of flux, it is nearly impossible to see the overall picture. True, companies make regular profit-and-loss reports to shareholders, but for government business these are based largely on the cash flow from Uncle Sam at the moment. (And this cash flow can be another significant reason for putting up with government bureaucracy.)

Stockholders, boards of directors, and top management rarely follow the history of contracts to their final completion, so the claims penalties, audits, engineering changes, unallowable costs, and renegotiations of alleged excess profits all get lost in the maze. Many times, it takes a major accounting effort to see how profitable any given award has been. Judgments are based on the cash flow of the minute. If that is good, the firm tends to ignore the ultimate contract profit return—which may not be known until a decade later.

· Government marketers can become "contractaholics." Like inveterate gamblers, they become more intent on

beating the system than on improving the ultimate earnings ratio. The complexities of marketing, the subtleties of
proposal writing, the skill of negotiation offer more than
enough challenge for the heartiest of contract gamblers,
who often feel that, like Everest, government contracts
must be tackled not for any profit they realize but just
because they are there. Corporate management must
watch out for marketing and contract negotiating
addicts—ultimate profits, not contract sleight-of-hand, determine a company's success.

· Finally, government business—whatever its profit per-
plexities—is hard to ignore because the potential is so
immense. Some firms make a killing. That alone is enough
to attract a steady influx of companies into the market. And
when the federal procurement system works—and even
during the many times when it doesn't work—company
officials believe they are able to make enough return to
justify selling to the government. The staggering number
of contract losers is offset by an equally astronomical total
of contract winners. And since businesspeople inherently
see themselves as winners, not losers, they continue to
court Uncle Sam in spite of all the profit uncertainties.

11

THE WINNER IS . . . .

How Agencies Evaluate
Your Proposal

• TRYING TO GUESS WHICH YARDSTICK THE CUSTOMER
USES TO MEASURE YOUR BID

• THE EVALUATION GAUNTLET:

Source evaluation board
Source selection board
Agency procurement authority
Higher government reviews

11. THE WINNER IS . . . .
How Agencies Evaluate Your Proposal

Contrary to legend, agencies do not pick contract winners with a Ouija board, although often it appears that way to disgruntled bidders. Most bids must run an elaborate legal gauntlet—a torturously slow process for contenders kept on tenterhooks waiting to hear who won.

Of course, an advertised IFB gives an immediate winner. The agency contract office sets the deadline day, calls all contenders, opens sealed bid envelopes, and the low price takes all—that's the law.

The bulk of bids—RFP and all variations of RFP—do not automatically go to the low bidder. In fact, the agency can award the contract to the high-price firm, and frequently does. The theory is that the government should get the best value, not just the least expensive product or service; or that the most competent vendor should be chosen to build a high-risk, complex project; or that the product that will cost less over its total lifetime should be selected.

This process, for better or for worse, works most of the time, but GAO files and Congressional reports are replete with RFP bid selections that didn't pan out. As noted, all too often Uncle Sam ends up choosing an expensive product that fails to work and frequently is delivered years late. This is scant comfort to disappointed losers who believe they were wronged in the government selection process. To understand the uncertainties and twists of fate in selling to Uncle Sam, one must know how most RFP bid winners are picked.

The government sets up an evaluation team for each bid, usually different persons from the battery of specialists and negotiators that confronted a company in initial bid discussion. They bring their own prejudices, points of view, and foibles—which may or may not be the same as those of the negotiators who wrangled over proposal minutiae. All the problems of the commercial buying committee are encountered. All the same preselling strategies apply. The difference is that in government marketing the vendor usually has no idea just who is on the evaluation team, hence the importance of selling the entire agency on the value of the project—those above and those below the project office.

The yardsticks used by source selection panels are as varied as the number of boards. One panel ranks technical expertise highest. Another ranks management strongest. All too often, the low price is still the governing factor. Public policy issues play a part. Source evaluation panels have chosen million-dollar contract winners on the basis of a promise to hire more minority workers. Hiring handicapped workers is another often considered factor.

Counterploy: If you can't determine the agency's evaluation yardstick from the RFP, hedge your bets by submitting alternate proposals, each keyed to a different evaluation criterion. One vendor submitted eighteen different proposals on the same bid, trying to be sure to cover all possible evaluation bets. Trying to stuff the bid ballot box doesn't guarantee your selection, but having to cope with a multitude of proposals may force reluctant agency project offices to do a better job next time in detailing more precisely the evaluation factors being used.

The simplest RFP competition is one evaluated only by the project office. Most agencies insist that the program director get technical, legal, and financial advice from aides, although in simple bids the program director is the acknowledged leader in final selection of the winner. In these situations, obviously, the better a firm knows the whims and fancies of the project leader, the better it can slant its proposal toward a favorable outcome. Prols can play this game as well as primes, because the single selection authority is used mainly for small, routine procurements of local agency offices that may be in the prol's home territory. The prol who is a Saturday afternoon golfing partner of the local project chief may be one up over the largest prime headquartered a thousand miles away.

Project office selections usually must be reviewed and approved by a higher agency authority. However, agency superiors are swamped by so many bid selection decisions pouring in from a myriad of local offices that they end up rubber-stamping most choices. This perfunctory review encourages some project offices to select pet vendors regardless of how other rivals bid. Even if challenged, a good buyocrat can conjure up suitable reasons to camouflage favoritism.

This system contains a special booby trap, especially for the unwary small firm. Some agencies encourage prols to bid to give an appearance of competition—and then end up awarding the contract to the favorite they had in mind all along.

Counterploy: Be wary if you are asked to bid on a project. Get all the intelligence you can. If you sense that the project office has tagged a winner before the bid proposals are in, don't bid. Firms on close enough terms with project officials may hint that they suspect what's going on but will bid to make a good show of competition—only if the firm is repaid by getting a better crack at the next bid.

Counterploy: Agency reorganizations and personnel shifts continually bring new faces into project offices, opening new chances to get a fairer shake in the future. New officials at higher levels in the agency can be told of a long history of favoritism on the part of a lower project office and may order a stop to it.

More complicated bids can follow any one of a number of evaluation steps, and winners are selected on any of a number of criteria. Newcomers to federal marketing are aghast at the widely varying practices in picking bid winners. One neophyte got two "Dear John" bid rejections in the same week from the same program office. First the firm was told that it rated highest on technical expertise, but that the low-price bidder had been selected. Two days later the firm got another rejection letter on a separate proposal stating that it was low-price bidder but that the award had gone to a rival judged to have a better technical proposal.

Agencies tend to remain vague on bid selection criteria, but procurement rules—backed up by GAO decisions—dictate that vendors should be given some idea of the yardstick used to evaluate their bids. These criteria must be specific and not couched in such broad, general terms as "primary factors" or "significant considerations." Vendors should complain to the project office when the RFP fails to spell out meaningful criteria. Frequently bidders are too timid to demand what procurement regs say is their right. If agencies then use convoluted logic to pick a winner, complacent contenders that allowed such vague criteria to stand get what they deserve.

Forcing agencies to spell out evaluation yardsticks is no panacea. Determined buyocrats can adjust any bid evaluation to meet factors listed in the RFP. GAO overturned an Army contract awarded on the basis of low price when the original RFP said that technical proposal and management were the most important factors. The Army merely reevaluated the proposals to pick the same firm—this time judging that the company had the best technical proposal.

Veteran marketers have come to expect such hodgepodge selections. They know that evaluation and selection have grown so complex, with so many sidetracks and reverse twists, that it is almost impossible to forecast the winner.

The typical federal bid selection can follow any or all of these steps:

1. Source Evaluation Board. One master panel can pore over bidder proposals to rank them technically and by cost, or proposals can be dissected with separate evaluation boards for technical, pricing, and management portions of the bids. The most complex bids may further divide up the technical proposal among several teams, each with its own area of expertise.

Playing Monday-morning quarterback on a source evaluation board is a futile exercise. GAO, Congress, and the courts seldom have the expertise to question the judgment of these officials except for the most flagrant departures from evaluation criteria.

2. Source Selection Board. An agency may use a separate source selection panel of top agency officials to review the opinions of the source evaluation boards and pick a winner. This panel is comprised of top agency brass, and its members have few qualms about overriding source evaluation board recommendations. If the agency front office executives know that the budget is tight or that the money for the project under bid is going to be diverted to other programs, they are quick to overrule a winner selected for higher priced technical superiority in favor of the drastically lower price bidder. One NASA center director vetoed the choice of a source evaluation board, fearing that the contractor would divert key employees already engaged in other projects for the center. One Army command wanted to standardize a vendor's computer for all battlefield uses and overruled a source evaluation board choice for another computer rated technically superior.

The closer the bid evaluation scores between contenders, the freer hand the source selection board has. When only a few evaluation points separate rivals who end the competition in a dead heat, no one can challenge whatever choice the higher selection panel makes. However, source selection boards are not loathe to reverse the evaluation panel, even in widely disparate rankings—good buyocrats can draw up a suitable justification that GAO and the courts will not question.

The mere existence of top agency source selection boards tends to compromise lower source evaluation boards. GS-17 and GS-18 middle-grade agency officials know the prejudices of their superiors, and it often takes heroism to make recommendations counter to the perceived agency party line. Some source evaluation panels have been overruled so often by superiors that a "what's the use?" attitude may degrade what should be an intensive bid review.

Not all agency bid selections suffer such abuses. At the other extreme, the source selection board merely rubber-stamps the source evaluation recommendations. That, after all, is the line of least resistance. Frequently, the evaluation board makes no clear-cut choice but presents superiors with a range of options. In these cases, the top board must make its decision based on the total agency situation.

Much has been written about the actual—or possible—influence on source selection authorities by powerful companies exerting political pressure. Only the naïve would assume that such influence never occurs. Selection by politics seems to ebb and flow in federal buying—a rash of press exposes turns agencies into moral purists; then, after a lapse, politicking during bid selection seems to rear its head again.

Influence peddling is a game only for the James Bonds of industry—for executives who don't fear eventually answering searing questions about their conduct before the TV lights of Congressional hearings. The overwhelming majority of project offices try to follow the rules, sometimes misguidedly, but honestly trying to resist undue political pressure. In any event, political influence is the preserve of privileged companies and possibly a few gambling primes. Most primes and all prols have no clout in this game.

3. The Head of the Agency or the Principal Deputy Signs off the Final Decision. Since front-office agency brass has probably had the strongest voice in the selection panel, this additional approval is usually superfluous. It does, however, give the agency one extra crack at delaying the bid, canceling it, or making some other eleventh-hour reversal. The agency chief who suddenly finds Congress has cut the agency's budget 15 percent may well refuse to sign or even send the whole bid back to be redesigned in light of an expected funding cut.

4. Other Reviews May Lie Ahead. The subordinate agency may come under a yet higher command or may be under a cabinet department. Various levels within these higher authorities may review the bid selection. Top department legal offices get into the act—a Commerce Department counsel overturned the subordinate agency chief's choice of a bid winner on technical legal grounds. The department comptroller can toss out all the months-long evaluation and selection review and make another recommendation stick. The Army comptroller refused to accept the choice of the technically superior bidder on a high-risk, sophisticated electronic eavesdropping system and directed that the award go to the low-price bidder because of Army budget shortages.

Some selections must be coordinated, if not approved, by interagency authorities such as GSA. This superagency almost never can change the selection, but it can challenge terms and conditions in the proposed contract award. Most superagencies simply rubber-stamp lower agency decisions—it's the easiest way out—but if a political hot potato surrounds the bid, superagency brass may protect their own flanks by insisting on special conditions or terms to be added to the contract. This rarely alters the original choice but adds further delay, extra complications, and in some cases, can even lead to cancellation of the bid at this late date.

The highest authority, the White House, has been known to impose its authority in the most politically sensitive contract awards. In the past, military aircraft were a popular target for White House intervention, and exposure of lesser abuses of the Watergate era revealed White House influence in contracts of the Commerce Department and other agencies.

The multilevel review of award selections has these dangers:

- Too many cooks may spoil the soup. A decision may be overturned at any level. At the very least, there is plenty of chance to delay, change, restructure, or cancel the entire project. Long-time federal contractors learn to expect surprises.

- Continual review at many levels delays final selection of a winner for weeks, even months. The more complex the project, the longer the wait. Smaller firms call the long, drawn-out selection process one of the most destructive parts of bidding. Contenders must line up a long list of possible suppliers in case they get the award, but trying to keep these suppliers on the hook, especially trying to keep their original bid prices firm, is often impossible. The bidder's own expenses pyramid during a protracted selection. To what bookkeeping account does a firm charge the cost of keeping engineering and design staffs together while waiting for bureaucrats to make up their minds?

The RFP may give an estimated date when award selection will be made, or project officials may informally give a deadline estimate—but the bidders on fixed-price contracts who take such officials at their word are in for trouble. If they price their bids expecting an award in the sixty to ninety days promised, they may suddenly find unexpected costs mounting while evaluation source selection drags on at a snail's pace.

The problems of the bid selection process should not frighten businesspeople out of the market. Companies should just be aware of what is going on and protect themselves as much as possible in drafting the bid proposal. (See Chapter 7, "Proposal Booby Traps: Pick Your Way Carefully.") The billions of dollars contracted each year to firms with fortitude to wait out the System make it worthwhile.

12
"I'VE BEEN ROBBED!"
The Art of Protesting

• **DON'T BE AFRAID TO STAND UP FOR YOUR RIGHTS**

• **WHERE TO TAKE YOUR COMPLAINTS (AND HOW TO USE THEM):**
The agency procurement contract office
Higher agency levels
Interagency groups
Your representative in Congress
The General Accounting Office
Federal courts
The press

12. "I'VE BEEN ROBBED!"
The Art of Protesting

It was a typical bid slug fest right down to the final bell. The contract was for $20 million computer terminals for the Air Force, but it could have been for any product. Four contenders waited on tenterhooks while the Air Force dragged on for months studying the bids, coming back with untold technical questions, twice asking everyone to extend bid prices another sixty days. Ages later, the three losers were notified that Company X had won the award. Marketing officials scurried down to the Air Force contract office to get a copy of the winning contract under the Freedom of Information Act. To their amazement, they saw that Company X had proposed a limited maintenance plan for the terminals for far less cost, and the Air Force had accepted this despite a far more extensive mandatory maintenance plan spelled out in the RFP.

The losing vendors shot off protests to the General Accounting Office, confident they had an ironclad case. In fact, they did. After eight months' study, GAO agreed that Company X's discount maintenance plan did indeed violate the terms of the RFP. Then the losers were in for a second jolt. GAO agreed to let the $20 million contract with Company X stand because work was so far along that the Air Force would lose time and money canceling the award, even with the illegal maintenance provision.

This case, which is all too common, shows the problems inherent in griping to Uncle Sam—the time it takes and the uncertainty of success. Of course, sore losers are rife in government selling. Most also-rans can conjure up some reason why they have been robbed in a bid selection, but protests can be more than sour grapes. They can involve anything from a simple difference of opinion to gross procurement violations.

If you have a grievance, the following are some suggestions to help you seek redress.

1. Don't Be Afraid to Press a Legitimate Complaint. Many firms feel they have been wronged but fail to protest for fear of agency retaliation. Buyocracy, of course, promotes this fear to keep com-

132

panies from protesting. But agency vengeance is largely a myth for many reasons:

- The number of protests has been mushrooming for years—agencies, the General Accounting Office, and the courts are getting cases at the rate of nearly four a day. A protester's big problem is not the threat of being singled out for retaliation; it is trying to get the government to find the complaint among the many buried in the system.

- Agencies have so much personnel turnover that few project officers are in their job several years later to take revenge on a protester, even if they want to.

- Agencies and program offices within agencies are often divided on how to handle any given procurement. Some may believe the protester is completely justified, even though others in the same office are fighting the protest. Such dichotomy protects the protester: too many officials may secretly agree with the protest to allow any retaliation.

Of course, some companies are known as chronic complainers, but agencies have learned from long experience how to neutralize these protests early in the game.

2. Complain to the Procurement Contract Office. This is the first, and surprisingly perhaps the best, place to complain—early! Protest as soon as possible against sole sources, fuzzy bid specifications, terms rigged in favor of competitors, or unfair treatment of your proposal during negotiations.

A company with an ironclad case may get the contract office to reverse itself and correct an injustice right there. After all, the worst fear of the procurement officials is getting reprimanded or admonished by superiors for an obvious miscue. Many diligent contract officers honestly want to correct mistakes that are pointed out to them. They also may fear that the complaining firm may protest to GAO, delaying an urgent bid while the government auditor ponderously reviews the case. In a few instances, fear of a protest may spur agencies to respond to a company gripe, but this is by no means certain. As we shall see, many agencies are so confident of being upheld by GAO that officials may ignore company threats.

Obviously, once a project office has selected a contract winner it's too late to protest here. Agency minds are made up. A small instrument firm once got the Air Force to cancel a contract that had been reserved for small business but was awarded to an undisputed big business. But this is rare. By the time a bid winner has been announced, protesters must go other routes.

3. Protesting to Higher Levels within an Agency Is Not Reliable. Officials tend to band together on any decision. After all, on big procurements the top levels of the agency have their necks on the line, too, because they approved a program office selection.

Paradoxically, opinions within agencies are often divided on thorny procurement issues. While top brass sticks together to uphold a lower level decision, other parts of the agency may secretly disagree with it. Companies with good pipelines into an agency can spot these potential allies. If they can't help on the current bid problem, they can perhaps influence future procurements that will be more to the company's liking.

Sometimes companies can profit from the appearance of a new employee within an agency. An eager new official has just been named to head up a vital division and wants to make his or her mark early. An obvious bidding injustice called to the official's attention may be seen as a chance to crack down on the agency troops and whip them into line. Unfortunately, such agency eager beavers are often worn down later by agency infighting. All too frequently, they get disgusted and quit the government entirely; but a smart vendor who catches a top agency go-getter at the zenith of enthusiasm may be able to get action on its complaint. A small auto parts supplier, tired of seeing the local military base buying office going repeatedly to the Big Four auto maker distributors sole-source, got procurement opened up for competitive bid by complaining to the new Army material procurement director, who wanted to make a quick example of a new policy stressing competition.

4. Take Your Case to Groups that Monitor Individual Agencies. Many times, the supergroups (interagency panels, General Services Administration) fall into line behind an agency decision and cannot be budged; but contractors can use the new-employee strategy here also—especially if the group has been looking for ways to make agencies toe the line or is just playing "Throw our weight around." These superpanels—once a firm knows which one monitors the agency in question—tend to be more approachable than the amorphous, fragmented, vast internal bureaucracy of most agencies. One or two key officials of the panels handle the problem in question, but such limited staff also means that the group is stretched thin, with only marginal time to devote to individual company protests.

5. Call in Your Representative in Congress. This may or may not help, depending on the position of the legislator. The legislator who sits on the key Congressional committee—better yet, the chair of the panel that controls the agency budget—can probably get buyocrats to jump when he or she questions a procurement. In the military bureaucracy colonels and captains are sensitive to contract questions from key members of Congress because these power figures can influence or veto some future appointments to general or admiral.

However, except for a few committee titans, Congressional power to reverse contract decisions is generally overrated. The typical legislator (or, more likely, a staff assistant) will fire off a hotly worded complaint to the agency in question or may even phone a key official of the agency to press the point. But if the lawmaker doesn't sit on a committee that controls agency purse strings, don't expect much. In most cases, the agency delays its answer and then the reply doesn't address the issues. It may be couched in government doublespeak. At the other extreme, the agency hurries back with volumes of highly complex details. Most legislators let it go at that, feeling they have done all they can to help a constituent. A few persistent ones may whip off a second challenge—only to get a similar bureaucratic evasion.

6. Protest through the General Accounting Office. This traditional protest route is probably the poorest. Of more than 1000 protests filed with GAO every year, less than 5 percent are ever upheld. Despite such Las Vegas odds, desperate companies see GAO as one of the few hopes they have in righting a bid injustice. It is probably the least costly procedure. A firm can draw up its own protest, although legal counsel would probably improve its case. A GAO protest has a cathartic effect for many an agitated executive. Middle management may protest to make a good show for its own front office or to vent top management heat.

Some contractors have more deliberate strategy behind their GAO protests. Even if the firm loses its protest, it may delay and foul up the bid at issue long enough to force the agency to come out with a completely new solicitation. Protests filed before a contract is awarded may force the agency to make requested changes voluntarily. Interior Department specifications for water flow monitors were a carbon copy of the data sheet for one firm's instrument, but the agency withdrew the disputed specs when a rival firm protested to GAO.

Firms also protest even when they expect to be rejected by GAO just to make the agency act more fairly on the next bid. GAO may only slap the agency's hands this time, but the government auditor may react more vigorously when the same questionable conduct occurs on the next bid.

GAO bid protest rules keep changing. Firms have a deadline to file protests; at this writing, they must file their complaint first with the contracting agency and then with GAO *within ten working days* after the alleged injustice has occurred. Any protests filed after this deadline are automatically thrown out, except for a few rare issues that GAO believes to be so important that it decides to take the case anyway. A protester doesn't need to file a fully documented case within the deadline time. A simple telegram with a bare sketch of the bid and issues in question will do. The protester then has a limited additional time to file in detail.

Now the protester is in for a surprise. He or she is under rigid deadlines, but the accused agency can take its time replying. In fact, the most common bureaucratic ploy is simply to take months to respond and make counterallegations while work continues under the contract at issue. By the time GAO finally does make a ruling, the decision is academic—the contract is nearly over. GAO claims it has no power to give agencies any deadline for replies, even to stop a contract under protest.

GAO will not challenge the technical evaluation of any agency, except for the most blatant violation of regulations. In most cases, GAO auditors claim they are not technically competent to question the myriad reasons that agencies give for protested buying actions. Military buyocrats regularly hide behind national security alibis, which GAO seldom questions. GAO almost always accepts a claimed urgent requirement as justification for sole-source procurement.

Even when GAO finds irregularities, all too often it slaps agency wrists but lets the questionable contract stand, as was the case with the Air Force computer terminal award cited at the beginning of this chapter. In another case, GAO ruled that the Army had illegally acquired computers worth $42 million but allowed most of the systems to remain because it would cost too much to replace the disputed computers.

In the rare instances in which GAO upholds a protest, the complaining firm must be sure that it does not win the battle and lose the business. A bus firm successfully overturned an Army award for base transportation service, only to see a new rival win the eventual rebid. A computer terminal firm won its protest, only to find the new contract award going to a second low-price bidder that the protester didn't even know was in the running.

There are many viable company strategies behind GAO protests—to bog down bids, put agencies on notice, get publicity—but trying to get GAO to overrule an agency is a long shot and should be treated as such.

7. Go through the Federal Court. This has proved the poorest remedy of [11] Injunctions to stop contracts while protests are being decided are rare. Justice is not blind—just unable to second-guess the technical expertise of agencies. Government lawyers can present reasons ranging from "national security" to "urgently needed equipment" to justify disputed actions. They inundate courtrooms with technical jargon. If a good project office has covered its tracks sufficiently, judges are loath to second-guess on technicalities except in cases that are patently fraudulent.

One exception: federal courts have been quick to champion the right of the public, including companies, to force agencies to disclose requested data under the Freedom of Information Act. While they are not strictly protests, Freedom of Information suits are used by knowledgeable firms to get documents, planning decisions, and reports behind a disputed agency action. Even if the firm is not able to use such inside information to turn the procurement around, the look behind the scenes tells how to be prepared for the next bid.

8. *The Press Is Often the Court of Last Resort.* The spotlight of publicity on a dubious action can shake many bureaucrats, embarrassing them or endangering their careers. At the very least, publicity creates the added work of writing endless reports to answer the charges to superiors and, perhaps, to Congress. Exposure in the trade press or consumer newspapers has often brought quick results when obscure protests to the agency or GAO have failed.

13

HOW TO LIVE WITH WHAT YOU BID
A Brief Guide to Contract Performance, Small Print, and Engineering Changes

- THE PREAWARD SURVEY: UNCLE SAM CHECKS YOU OUT

- USING CONTRACT CHANGES TO YOUR ADVANTAGE

- HOW TO DEAL WITH INSPECTIONS, TESTING AND MORE TESTING, SLOW PAYMENTS

- WATCH YOUR WARRANTIES—THEY CAN COME BACK TO HAUNT YOU

13. HOW TO LIVE WITH WHAT YOU BID
A Brief Guide to Contract Performance, Small Print, and Engineering Changes

A long-awaited phone call, or an official notice picked up at the agency contracting office: You won. Champagne corks pop; the joy flows in wild celebration of the win. But hardly has the last hurrah died than you find not all is roses. Almost every government contract victory carries with it an assortment of problems and potential trouble spots. Veteran firms accept the chaff with the wheat, starting from the very beginning to mitigate troubles. Newcomers are often surprised to find what they thought was a competitive triumph backfiring on them in a hundred different ways.

Consider the jubilant five-person painting firm that won the bid to paint nine buildings at a New York Air National Guard center. The contractor submitted paint samples to the program office, and when he got no reply in a month, checked back. Another month went by while the bureaucracy tried to find out what happened to the paint samples. Finally, it was discovered that the samples were sent back—not to the contractor, but to the mystified paint companies themselves, who threw away the unintelligble Air Force communication. More months were required to get the paint samples okayed. When the contractor finally started work on the long-delayed project, Air Force inspectors got into a dispute over whether the blue tone was actually the blue specified. The Air Force held up progress payments and the disgruntled contractor stopped work. Letters went back and forth for nine months between the project office and the contractor. Finally, an agreement was reached and work resumed more than a year after the original contract was awarded. The contractor ran into bad weather and asked for a hold during the winter. The Air Force agreed if there is no increase in price. The next spring, when work was to resume, the contractor was booked solid with other jobs and asked for another extension. After another two months the Air Force terminated the contract and went out for bids again. Two and a half years after the original, simple contract to paint nine buildings had been awarded, the work had still not been completed.

PREAWARD SURVEY—HERE'S LOOKING AT YOU

Even before the contract is signed, the selected firm gets its first taste that all may not be pure gravy. The agency contract administrators descend en masse on corporate offices to scrutinize company management, examining everything from travel expenses to insurance to buying plans to corporate financing. Since a company's management proposal—and to some extent its technical and cost proposals—plowed the same ground, concerned executives understandably wonder why entirely new, exhaustive surveys must be made. But this is a new team of agency officials—the contract administrators as opposed to the proposal evaluators and contract officer. They must do their thing also to assure that the contractor can live up to what it promised in the proposal.

The winning vendor may get surveyed not once but several times before it can start work. The firm also gets surveyed anew on almost every contract it wins. Rationally, it would seem that once government contract administrators have dissected a firm for one program, the same report card would hold up for other contracts won in subsequent months. But agencies are afraid of being called on the carpet for not surveying a vendor, no matter how many surveys have been run previously. So the System grinds relentlessly on, with no way to stop it, survey after survey, every time a contract is let.

Later the firm will be dissected by government auditors, various investigators, and, if it is in the aerospace and defense business, perhaps Renegotiation Board examiners. All these probers, to one degree or another, are plowing over the same company books, the same company records and procedures. Disgruntled company officers can be excused for wondering why one branch does not talk to another and why one auditing call cannot do for all.

Defense contractors come under double scrutiny. Each military service has its own contract administrators survey the winner. In addition, the Department of Defense has centralized inspection in a combined Defense Contract Administration Agency, whose regional officials will also survey a firm.

Privileged firms and veteran primes have been through the exercise so many times that it becomes a ritual with each side making expected responses. Prols and small firms, on the other hand, may come under microscopic inspection by administrators. Actually, good agency administration officials can be a help to inexperienced contractors. They can point out potential flaws in a firm's procedures and recommend management controls that could save future headaches. Of course, contract administrators can fall victim to the temptation of trying to run the contractor's business, and since they themselves are not responsible for a bottom-line profit, they can come up with many schemes that bear close scrutiny.

Many types of federal contracts bring an immediate demand: the firm must secure a bond equal to the amount of the contract as surety for its performance. Construction contracts, some service work, and turnkey projects from airport control towers to electrical generating stations usually require a performance surety bond. Prols must be certain they can secure bonds, for the government will not let work start without them despite a contract's being signed. Precious time can be lost trying to line up a surety bond, but the government will still hold the firm to the contract completion date.

The bond can become just another of the many battlegrounds in later contract disputes. An aggrieved firm taking a dispute to court often must post bond for the total price in contention, a figure often too high to make a court case feasible. One firm had completed its contract but had claims against the agency, which refused to consider them unless the firm took out a new surety bond for the entire amount of the completed project. Later, when the contractor won the claims fight, the agency refused to pay the cost of the extra surety bond demanded.

Another early problem is the "half-win" for a contractor. Instead of getting a definite, full-fledged contract, the company gets a "letter contract"—a commitment from the agency to start work, with definite prices and contract details to be agreed on at a later date. A letter contract usually signals that the contractor and the agency could not come to terms during the usual precontract negotiations or that the agency's project is still so vague that binding contract terms were impossible at the time the winner was selected. Letter contracts merely extend the "now I've got you" pricing and terms negotiating battle well into the contract period—with the added sport that work is already going on while company and bureaucrats are dickering over the cost. The privileged firms are often able to use letter contracts as open-ended blank checks until the government can finally get contract pricing nailed down in a definitive pact. Even alert primes can work to slip as much unexpected cost increase as possible into the final negotiated contract price.

CONTRACT CHANGES: NOTHING IS AS CONSTANT AS CHANGE

The early stages of a contract are filled with surprises. The unwary winner discovers that those hundreds of pages of boilerplate clauses do mean something. Any one of the innocent canned terms can suddenly surface to confound the winner. One firm supplying 36,000 blankets to the Army was informed in the first week that it had agreed to ship each blanket in individual 22- by 38-inch packages, not one inch different in either dimension. The Armed Services Contract Appeals Board agreed that the clause was minor but said a contract is still a contract and the supplier must fulfill the terms to which it had agreed, no matter how innocently.

Early in the game the winner also may get unexpectedly deficient government engineering drawings, parts lists, and specifications. Of course, a full technical description of the project should have been in the original bid solicitation, but frequently these drawings and specs are shot full of holes, giving bidders a major proposal headache. All too often, drawings for major subsystems are promised later after the contract has been awarded. Many times, when bids are originally invited, Uncle Sam is locked in a legal battle with the original subsystem developer for the data package and cannot deliver specifications until that dispute is resolved. All too often, the agency is inventing a project the entire time a bid is underway. When the contract is awarded, revised drawings and data—often faulty—are dumped on the winning contractor.

Bad drawings set up a legal tiff between company and government. The contractor claims that extra funding is due to make the deficient drawings work. The agency disputes what changes are needed. If a firm has little leverage in such a fight, it may be forced to wait through years of litigation to recover extra costs of reworking bad government specs and data.

Caution: A contractor can recommend changes to faulty specs and be thrown into a no-win dilemma by agency indecision. Until a contracting office definitely agrees to any change, the company is expected to continue working on the original contract terms and specs. Otherwise, it may be guilty of default. But if original contract drawings are so defective that an unusable product or service results, the contractor may face a long claims fight to prove that the fault is the government's and not the contractor's. Faulty specs can be serious. One ammunition manufacturer suffered five plant explosions because Army directions for mixing powders into pellets were wrong.

On the other hand, faulty drawings can be a golden opportunity to mine a contract for all it's worth—and then some. Even prols may be able to play this strategy if they have good contract negotiators. The contractor prevails upon the agency program office to change the original contract—both the work statement and corresponding price—to correct the deficient drawings. In the jargon of the business, these become ECPs—engineering change proposals.

An ECP reopens contract negotiations. No matter how ironclad the price and terms of the original pact are, an ECP to remedy a government mistake gives the contractor a second bargaining chance, which can shift bargaining power to the contractor. Now Uncle Sam is at fault and must fairly quickly revise the contract to overcome original design inadequacies.

A smart contractor tries to recover any prior contract losses. If the firm bid an unusually low price or bought into the contract, ECPs allow it to get new, higher prices. The likelihood of deficient specs somewhere in a government project is so great that many firms routinely bank on ECPs to rewrite contracts after they are originally negotiated. ECP is the standard bail-out of a buy-in. (See Chapter 8, "Winning at Any Price.")

Sometimes agencies get obstinate and refuse to allow ECPs to overcome alleged design faults. The Defense Communication Agency refused to allow any changes in a particularly bad data terminal design, so the contractor built the device precisely according to DCA drawings. It failed miserably, and the agency used the company's proposed ECP as the specs for a new competitive bid. Not unexpectedly, the original vendor won that bid also, at a far higher price than the originally proposed ECP.

Caution: Be sure to get the agency contract office to agree in writing to any ECP. Too many contractors go ahead with extensive rework on only an oral commitment, then sadly learn they cannot get paid because no written, legal agreement was made. Government officials, in a pinch to get a product delivered on time, often pressure contractors to go ahead with ECP work, claiming written approval will be forthcoming. Beware. Definite contract approval may be a long time coming, and in a few cases agencies have later denied ever authorizing such changes. Be sure to follow all the legal nitty-gritty. One firm submitted a proposed ECP on DOD Form 633-5, when it should have used DOD Form 633-5 Revised. The firm went ahead with expensive changes with assurances that its request would be approved. A year later, the firm was told that it had used the wrong form and must resubmit its request. By this time, the bargaining strength had shifted to Uncle Sam, who used it to beat the company down to a far lower price for the ECP.

Be sure to document completely all the extra expenses involved in a government-ordered ECP. Frequently buyers balk at paying the full ticket, and firms that cannot make a strong case to agency appeals boards may end up footing much of the extra cost themselves. A clothing manufacturer got a rush change in its contract to help it make deliveries of 26,175 topcoats for the Army in ninety days—but the Armed Services Contract Appeals Board denied the firm's claim for $71,500 in extra costs because it claimed the company did not prove any damage.

Agencies love to ask contractors for a lot of change proposals, just as they ask for frequent bid proposals that are left in limbo. Contractors can waste valuable time and funds costing out complex engineering changes that are never accepted. The Navy asked an aircraft firm to price out thirty-five requested ECPs on a major aircraft but accepted only one.

Know what you are signing on any ECP. Engineering changes requested by the government can be as complex and involved as the original bid solicitation, written in unintelligible legal jargon. One small firm president thought he was just signing a form acknowledging that he had received a change order on a contract. He had actually signed an agreement to do the work on very unfavorable terms and conditions. When he later objected to the terms, he was told that he had already signed an agreement on the disputed conditions.

Be sure, if delivery dates are extended through a change order, that target deadlines for extra-incentive bonuses in the contract are also extended. A pipefitting contractor was happy to get the completion date of its Air Force contract extended by forty-five days—but lost a $90,000 incentive bonus because the bonus target deadline was not adjusted to the new delivery date.

When Uncle Sam seeks to change the original contract, smart firms try to milk the change for all they can get. Most changes imply that extra time will be needed to make the change, whether it is adding a complex guidance system to a missile or simply adding extra heating ducts to a housing project. Shrewd contractors will negotiate new delivery dates that give them all the fudge factor they need, and then some, compared to tight completion deadlines they may have been forced to sign under competitive pressure in the original bid. One firm making fuel tanks found that Air Force drawings for welds were faulty and that new joints and flanges had to be added to correct the trouble. The firm now found itself in the negotiating driver's seat, so it forced the Air Force to mark its company brand-name parts as "required" on the engineering drawings. Thus, if any new bids for fuel tanks came out, the firm had a locked-in position through the drawings specifying its parts.

Of course, the contractor may instigate an ECP to remedy its own troubles on a project, to seek a bail-out for a buy-in, to get extra time to complete the contract. Any firm, from privileged to prol, may be able to force through changes. Even the lowliest company supplying a critical part that the program office can get nowhere else can play this game. Better yet, the company can get the agency to make the needed changes as if they had been requested originally by the government. A hundred different reasons can be given: change in scope of the program, new capabilities being added, capabilities being reduced, shift in quantities ordered. Redirection of the program, changing requirements, and so on. One interesting doublethink from the Army justified a $70 million change to modify a communication switch to make it more austere and less complex in order to save money.

Troubled contractors score a real coup when they cajole the customer into substituting a patchwork of older equipment when they can't make original contract designs. One large communications firm failed after three years and $13 million spent to build a microwave radio for the Air Force. A prol or some primes would have been terminated long before three years had gone by, but this privileged contractor convinced the Air Force to let it piece together a radio out of older modules—and got another $5 million to try again.

Congress, higher agency officials, and the General Accounting Office rarely have the expertise to challenge a well-conceived cover story for ECPs to bail out a troubled contractor. Only when a project falls into real trouble that requires a series of ECP bail-outs do changes become so blatant that higher authorities crack down.

Contractors must know their customer intimately to be sure buyers will cooperate on ECP relief. Project offices may refuse and hold companies to their original terms—or default the firm if it cannot deliver. Prols that do not have a strong bargaining position find it tough to get beneficial changes.

Just as contractors try to wrest extra advantage from ECPs, Uncle Sam also uses midcontract changes to force extra concessions from suppliers. Firms only seeking an extension for delivery dates may find the project office using the opportunity to put in extra demands not in the original contract. Contractors desperate to get an extended completion date often are forced to agree to other demands.

Sometimes contractors are hit hard in the pocketbook by contract changes over which they have little control. A program office suddenly loses most of its funding and is forced, midway through the program, to cut back drastically on quantities ordered or on product sophistication. However, a firm has committed itself to long-range production, financing, material acquisition, and labor-hiring plans, which now must be rejuggled in midstream. Unless a firm has signed away its rights in such changes, it has a good case for collecting damages from Uncle Sam, but this is often more easily said than done. More than one firm has been forced to endure a five- to eight-year court fight to get reimbursed for such costs. (See Chapter 16, "Claims and Other Squatter Rights.")

When budgets are especially tight, agencies may try to force suppliers to change cost-plus contracts to fixed-price pacts. Sometimes they get the same result simply by forcing contractors to agree to a ceiling price on a cost-plus pact. A firm that priced an original proposal with the idea of being reimbursed for most project costs is in a bad position when it suddenly finds itself working under a fixed price midway through the contract.

INSPECTORS: BIG BROTHER IS WATCHING YOU

Other problems, such as inspectors, prove that winning the contract isn't everything in dealing with Uncle Sam. On large contracts Uncle Sam has inspectors right inside the plant to watch every move. Usually the in-plant inspector is not an adversary and may actually be a distinct help in untangling unexpected production problems. The caliber of these government in-plant inspectors can vary widely, however, with less capable officials being difficult to work with at best and at worst stirring up trouble back at the agency program office.

Caution: Even though in-plant government inspectors are in direct, day-to-day contact with a firm, they have no authority to approve contract changes or commitments. In the urgency to get production problems solved, resident inspectors will often pressure contractors to make recommended changes, claiming, "I'll take care of it back at the program office." But only the official program contract officer can legally approve any change, and the contract officer may overrule the in-plant inspector, or, more likely, simply avoid making any decision. In either case, the contractor risks ending up footing any extra expense without written contract officer approval. *Be sure to get all changes approved in writing from the legal contract authority— usually the contracting office.* Verbal approval from anyone in the government—even the contracting officer—won't stand up if agency officials later refuse to honor the change. Also, don't make changes unilaterally, even if it saves Uncle Sam money, without contracting office approval. A construction firm didn't install costly, highest sensitivity water sprinkler heads in noncombustible areas of Navy warehouses, using an acceptable industry-grade sprinkler instead. The claims board forced the firm to redo the job at its own expense, saying, "Although the contractor's intentions to save money are laudable, if the government desires to use sledge hammers to drive nails, it is the government's prerogative."

Firms frequently get caught in a maze of conflicting reports at various government levels. The in-plant inspector says one thing; the agency contract administration office, another; the agency project office has yet a third opinion. More differences may be voiced later by government auditors and a host of specialized inspectors, ranging from military security offices to labor inspectors. The beleaguered contractor learns that one group of government inspectors rarely communicates with the others, so it may be getting widely varying directives and recommendations. On the very same day one firm got a notice from Labor Department inspectors that it was paying below the prevailing wage rate in the area to its service workers and was told by the contracting office that its labor costs were excessive and must be adjusted downward.

Sometimes inspection-happy bureaucrats thwart and interfere with a contractor's work on a project. A structural steel firm could hardly complete bridge supports because of the constant government inspection visits—more than 725 during the life of the contract. Agencies will probably insist on an inspection contract clause that will allow them to conduct in-plant inspections at any time, but contractors should insist on another clause that such inspections do not disrupt work.

Many government project offices have so little expertise that they must hire consultants or outside firms to monitor a contractor's work. The supplier must now quickly learn the prejudices and foibles of still another evaluator. Unfortunately, the consultant may have a different concept of the program than the agency that awarded the contract initially. Often the outside consultant and government auditors have contradictory opinions, and the contractor is caught in another vise.

With so many contract monitors within the government, suppliers find themselves giving program review after program review. One level of an agency challenges another or, to assert its authority, raises countless questions on the program progress. The contractor makes a command performance review, flying key technical, management, and contract executives to government offices. The time needed to prepare, rehearse, and give a day-long briefing ties up precious hours of working time, runs up expenses, and strains company resources. Uncle Sam usually ends up paying the bill, but the frequent interruptions can tax contractors' ability to keep projects on schedule. Since each succeeding briefing often repeats the same show for a new audience, vendors ponder the value of such reruns. Actually, briefings and program reviews make many bureaucrats feel more comfortable. Frequently the diversions and excuses served up by contractors on a troubled project are grabbed by the buyers being briefed to be used on their superiors.

> *Strategy:* Tell buyers only what they want to hear in briefings. Privileged firms and primes can claim that solutions to serious technical problems are "in hand." Cost tradeoff studies are being made to lessen the impact of expected contract price increases. Development costs are spiraling, but this is to hold the price for eventual production. Such doublespeak is talking the language of buyocrats, but prols beware: buyocracy will cut you short every time you try to smokescreen problems.

SLOW PAY: DUNNING UNCLE SAM

It comes as a shock to many contract newcomers that the U.S. government can be delinquent in paying its bills; but red tape, interagency disputes, bureaucratic bumbling, and sometimes deliberate holding up of checks to ease strained agency budgets can cause tardy payments. Small firms that have borrowed heavily to perform on government contracts are caught in a financial pinch. But even if Uncle Sam's slow payments force a firm to extend its loans, the government steadfastly refuses to pay the extra interest.

To get your payments on time, you must be sure to fill out every invoice and government form in precisely the prescribed manner—dot all *i*'s and cross all *t*'s just the way the agency demands. Include any documentation or requested supporting material. Otherwise, your company may suffer long payment delays while layers of bureaucrats scrutinize an invoice with slight omissions—and finally, months later, send it back to be filled out again. Unwary companies may not even know that their checks are held up in the bureaucratic limbo. Trying to trace through the maze of federal accounting bureaucracy to locate a delayed payment can be a nightmare. Sometimes firms are simply innocent victims of bureaucratic mixups. One contracting officer—the only person able to authorize payment—put a small firm's invoice in his safe in the flurry of leaving for a six-month sabbatical in India. The desperate contractor never was able to find the missing invoice and did not get final payment until the official returned.

Strategy: You can use Uncle Sam's slow pay to your advantage: give the government a big prompt-payment discount, which can make your proposal economically attractive in the bid evaluation. It's a gamble, but the program office so frequently drags out payment that odds are good that you will never have to give the discount.

KEEPING UP WITH PROGRESS PAYMENTS

Contractors get regular biweekly or monthly progress payments from Uncle Sam while they are performing government work. Firms submit validated invoices for the money they have spent during the period and are reimbursed by the government contract office. The theory is that it costs Uncle Sam less to put contracts on a pay-as-you-go basis than it does to force firms to borrow the full amount needed to complete the work.

This is supposed to make government business less capital-intensive than other markets. Contractors are supposed to be working on Uncle Sam's money, not their own. Actually, since agency negotiating strategy is to unload as much risk onto contractors as possible, companies end up using more of their own funds than the government cares to admit. If firms are forced to borrow these funds, the government refuses to pay most interest expense. Recently the government changed its policy to allow interest on borrowing for capital equipment, recognizing that without such reimbursement, contractors had little incentive to invest their own funds in more efficient, modern equipment.

Progress payments are usually—but not always—paid routinely. Contractors and project offices can get into a squabble over the validity of an invoice. Sometimes a contract office will hold up progress payments or deduct amounts claimed to be due the government if there is a dispute on contractor performance. Some contracts do not allow progress payments to start until a product passes an initial acceptance test. Be careful: Delayed government testing or a dispute on test results or other details can hold up progress payments for months or years. One test instrument firm could not get progress payments for two years; even though the

Army liked the product, it would not approve the user's manual that came with the item.

TESTING . . . TESTING . . .

Most contracts require a product or service to pass inspection before it is accepted. Almost always, the initial production unit must be approved—called "first article testing"—before any further shipments can be made. After that, the contract office may make only spot sample inspections or may make a 100 percent inspection of all items delivered.

> *Caution:* Be sure the contract spells out how inspection tests are to be made and what test equipment will be used. The Navy rejected a sophisticated missile warhead from one firm because inspection gauges showed flaws in the casing. The contractor was shocked because its own plant inspection had revealed no faults. The company spent a fortune trying to correct the alleged flaws before it discovered that Navy inspectors were using faulty gauges. In another case, Army inspectors improperly tested rifle barrels and allowed rust to form. The firm was forced to do costly extra work on the rifles and had to fight a three-year claims battle to get a portion of the extra cost back.

WATCH YOUR WARRANTIES

Bureaucrats, like any other customers, love product warranties. Such guarantees are extremely difficult to write for government business. Products can be used—or misused—by inept government workers. Sophisticated equipment can be stored carelessly or mishandled in shipment. Warranties must be carefully drafted to exempt the manufacturer from all conceivable equipment abuses. Frequently buyers who know full well that the government is at fault will still try to force a firm to make good on its warranty, holding out the lure of future orders or, conversely, threatening contract cancellation.

> *Strategy:* Some warranties are not as risky as they might appear. Products often sit in government warehouses for years before they are sent out for use. Sometimes the war-

ranty period has expired before a federal customer ever gets around to using the product.

Be explicit in all warranties included in contracts. Avoid ambiguous clauses that are easy to misinterpret. Don't say: "Workmanship shall be of such high grade to ensure satisfactory operation consistent with service life." Spell out exactly what product performance is guaranteed in precisely the manner it is used over a definite lifetime.

Don't say, "The valve shall allow no leakage." Describe the test conditions and performance parameters used to judge any valve leakage; otherwise, the government customer may run faulty tests—and you end up replacing perfectly good valves that were simply abused in testing.

Watch undefined terms. "Nominal performance" means different things to different people. You may end up in long legal hassles—and you may lose—when program offices claim that "nominal performance" was not achieved. Loose terms such as "design goal" are open to later dispute. For example, a contractor claims that "design goal" just means the firm makes its best effort to reach a target, but the customer claims that it is a definite goal that must be met to fulfill the warranty.

Insist on contract clauses that will protect you. A standard clause says: "If the government does not reject a test report on the product being procured within thirty days of the submitted postmarket date, the test will be deemed approved." This guards against program offices stalling for months—or even a year—only to conclude that tests run long ago did not fulfill the warranty. Bureaucracy often gets so tangled up that program officials don't examine test reports within thirty days, so contractors with such protective clauses get an almost automatic approval of test results.

Problems do crop up on government contracts. Alert vendors, however, act quickly to keep small problems from erupting into major disasters. Knowing how to put out contract brush fires can be more valuable than all the company's technological expertise.

14
PAPERWORK
How to Keep from Being Buried

• COPING WITH MOUNTAINS OF PAPER IN GOVERNMENT CONTRACTS

• SOME PARTICULAR PAPER PROBLEMS:
Truth in negotiation
Cost accounting standards
Data rights

14. PAPERWORK
How to Keep from Being Buried

The chief output of any government contract is paper. Tons of it. Whatever else is produced in the contract almost seems incidental to the torrents of paperwork. An aerospace contractor once tried to measure the sheer mass of reports, data, forms, reviews, documentation, and certification on just one project—and found that the stack of paperwork done in a year topped the 127-foot length of the missile being developed.

Paperwork, of course, keeps armies of bureaucrats employed, although contractors suspect that even the massive civil service work forces cannot possibly sift through the mountains of data and documentation on every project. Paperwork also builds empires for contractors, who prepare the exhaustive data demanded. Companies may grumble, but as long as Uncle Sam pays the cost, contractors readily acquiesce in this Unholy Paperwork Alliance.

Pyramids of paper act as bureaucratic security blankets. Even if they can't sift through the endless mass, buyers have protected their flanks from political attack. If Congress or GAO or agency superiors raise any questions, the answers are sure to be buried somewhere in the mass. If nothing else, there are more than enough documents to divert any outside probers or discourage them from continuing their search.

The larger the contract, the more paperwork is required, but even simple, mundane procurements can be weighted down with myriads of report forms. Veteran government marketers have learned a few general rules for coping with the paper avalanche:

Report All Data Accurately and Completely. Don't skimp, no matter how great the temptation or how much of a nuisance the reports are—as long as Uncle Sam pays. Even if bureaucrats only spot-check documents, the reports and forms chosen for review must be correct in every detail. If the government contract office demands a complete test report on every single component—NASA has asked for such a pedigree on every one of 178,000 parts in a spacecraft—give it in copious detail. If the office wants a weekly report on the delivery status of every component in the project, make out a detailed schedule. Omissions, shoddy data, or errors can touch off a full-scale government review. If a contract runs into any trouble spots—and there are few that do not develop some strains—faulty reporting can knock out any leverage the firm has in negotiating remedial action.

If a Contract Has Any Problems, Don't Lie in Reports. Adopt the buyocrats' own doublespeak. One Fortune 500 company felt honesty was the best policy and forthrightly warned the customer that the program was facing a 40 percent cost growth. The contract was terminated shortly afterward. A competitor on a comparable project for the same agency weasel-worded about similar cost problems. This firm kept its contract and later got successful funding increases that doubled the original contract price.

Tell Customers What They Want to Hear. If subcontracting to minority business is getting a bureaucratic push, stress what is being done to bring in minority firms. If "design to cost" or "life cycle cost" is the current procurement fashion, go into copious detail on how such concepts are being implemented on the contract.

Play the Game According to the Rules. Agencies have evolved elaborate management reporting schemes with exotic names such as PERT (program evaluation and reporting technique); configuration management; cost schedule control system. All are designed to solve the Pandora's box of troubles that can afflict complex government projects and work to varying degrees. Neophyte contractors need not panic. Uncle Sam has volumes of instructions for setting up such systems. Consultants, trade associations, and contract administrators can be hired to help a firm set up whatever management system is demanded.

The common feature of all these systems is torrents of paperwork. The purpose of any management system is to keep a program on track and to allow agencies to keep watch on contractors. This demands prodigious reports and complex flow diagrams that show the status of all parts of the program and how they interrelate.

None of these management systems is a cure-all. Despite continual refining, many big government programs still run into trouble, suffer horrendous cost overruns, and flounder in long program slippages. Ironically, contractors on these very snarled projects continue to pour out detailed PERT or configuration management reports that are supposed to prevent such problems. While company contract administrators dutifully make routine cost schedule control system reports, teams from the agency are working on emergency radical changes at the contractor plant.

The management systems and their train of reports tend to take on a life of their own, almost beyond the very programs they are supposed to control. The danger is that both contractors and project offices become so enamoured with the paperwork systems that report upon report is coming out on schedule while real-world problems are going unsolved.

> *Rule:* Paperwork is no substitute for good contract management, both on the part of the contractor and the government. Management systems and associated reports, like any tool, are no better than the people who use them.

Be Sure Uncle Sam Pays the Full Cost of Paperwork. As long as the agency foots the expense, the contractor faces only the nuisance of endless reporting. Unfortunately, firms all too often forget the high cost of fulfilling buyocracy's appetite for paper and don't include this major expense in their bid prices. Or federal agencies can impose massive new paperwork requirements midway through a fixed-price contract, and suppliers may end up having to foot the extra cost themselves.

> *Caution:* Boilerplate contract requirements frequently hide paperwork demands. Be sure to include them in the contract price. A truck distributor found that it had agreed in a boilerplate clause to furnish a full parts list for each truck ordered by the Army. A test instrument manufacturer discovered that one innocent-looking clause required the firm to submit regular updated and completely revised parts lists to all Air Force users of the equipment; the unexpected extra cost nearly wiped out all contract profits.

Paperwork can zap vendors with unexpected costs in other ways. Rejected forms, challenged reports, and misinterpreted documents mean costly rewriting. Worse yet, inadequately completed forms may languish for months in the bureaucracy getting no action at all. If the paper snarl involves money for the contractor, the incomplete form or report can hurt—badly.

Small firms, especially, are ill-equipped to handle critical documents. One four-person firm lost a chance to appeal an adverse program office decision that cost it $6700 because the agency document arrived while the president was home ill. By the time he returned to his desk, the time limit for appeal had expired.

Caution: Fill out every form as carefully as you do your tax return. It may end up costing you more money. One program office held up progress payments to a firm for three months because the standard form requesting payments was incorrectly filled out. Yet the frantic contractor was not able to find anyone in the agency who could furnish the information that this was the reason for the firm's not getting paid.

So far, we have been dealing with general rules that apply to almost all government paperwork, but there are unique paper monsters that require special attention. Flubbing any of these sacrosanct paperwork demands can be devastating.

TRUTH IN NEGOTIATION

Public Law 87-653 (Truth in Negotiation) was enacted in 1962 because Congress feared that contractors were not being fully honest on proposed prices during negotiations with government. Lawmakers were concerned that a firm would sign a contract, then find ways to cut its costs and pocket the savings as extra profit. That is a no-no under Truth in Negotiation, which allows Uncle Sam to charge defective pricing in the original contract and pocket the savings.

Truth in Negotiation applies only to certain contracts, some of the largest in the government. Negotiated contracts above $100,000 in the Department of Defense, NASA, and the Department of Energy are covered, although the threshold dollar value can be lowered or raised slightly by administrative order, depending on politics at the moment.

Under this law, contractors are supposed to complete a detailed government form, certifying that all prices negotiated with the government are "accurate, complete, and timely." Often the bidder must back this up with extensive documentation showing how the prices in each part of the proposal were determined.

There are some loopholes. A firm can refuse to fill out the required form to certify its bid prices. Usually that automatically results in the agency throwing out the bid, but if the bidder has a clear upper hand in negotiations (it is the sole supplier) and if all other competitors also refuse to certify prices, the government customer can waive the Truth in Negotiation requirement. At this writing, the oil industry has backed government agencies against the wall because all suppliers refuse to sign Truth in Negotiation forms. Since agencies need oil, the requirement is routinely waived for petroleum contracts.

A firm that is forced to certify its cost and pricing data under Truth in Negotiation must check and recheck all parts of its price down to the lowest subcontractor level. Any sudden cost reduction on any part of the program could bring an army of government auditors descending on the company books. A turbine manufacturer was charged with defective pricing on eight small parts on a $3 million contract because the parts had come from company inventory at a lower cost than prices the firm had quoted the government.

Watch careless estimates in preparing bid prices. A building air-conditioning contractor made a quick estimate of what major parts would cost based on existing work the firm was doing. After the firm was awarded the contract, it was able to get major components $22,000 cheaper from suppliers. Eagle-eyed government auditors spotted the savings and deducted $22,000 from the contract funding for "defective pricing."

One small concession to contractors is that the government is now forced to balance any defective price "savings" pocketed by the firm against cost overruns the company had to bear on other parts of the contract—but companies had to go to court to win even this grudging concession.

Truth in Negotiation throws another monkey wrench at prime contractors—they are responsible for making sure that their subs certify all their prices. Of course, no subcontractor is going to open its books to another firm, one that is a possible competitor on another bid. So the prime has little power to assure that subcontractor certified prices are accurate; yet, the prime is zapped if subcontractor prices are later charged to be defective. To satisfy the law, subcontractors can submit cost data directly to the government, bypassing the prime. However, if federal auditors spot any price discrepancy in the sub, they can collect from the prime, despite the fact that the prime has never seen the sub's cost records.

Unfair? Probably, but buyocracy has a stock answer: "Tell it to the (claims court) judge." There is one consolation for businesspeople—Truth in Negotiation disputes tend to be very small, although some claims can be substantial and wipe out any profit earned. But even if a firm never suffers a defective pricing claim, if it is subject to Truth in Negotiation coverage, it faces an onslaught of paperwork to justify every minute part of its bid pricing.

COST ACCOUNTING STANDARDS

There's another paperwork surprise for firms that have defense or aerospace negotiated contracts for more than $500,000. These firms must file a galaxy of accounting reports prescribed by the government under special cost accounting standards. Consult your accountant; only experts can fathom the detailed pronouncements, dictating how you must keep your financial records for these contracts.

Companies that do only a smattering of negotiated defense or aerospace business usually must keep two sets of books, one for their regular business and one for contracts subject to government cost accounting standards. Contractors may be selling identically the same product to different government agencies but must keep their books on the contracts separate if one agency is subject to cost accounting standards and the others are not.

The defense and aerospace accounting standards are at odds with other government accounting rules, such as the Internal Revenue Service, the Renegotiation Board, the Customs Service, and agency internal regulations. At this writing, the cost accounting standards do not allow accelerated depreciation write-offs on negotiated contracts, although other types of defense or aerospace contracts and the IRS allow such depreciation. The accounting rules for negotiated contracts force firms to figure pension plan costs differently than do IRS and the Labor Department.

This jumble of accounting rules doubles and triples the paperwork load. Each part of government adamantly sticks by its own rules.

Veteran contractors have begrudgingly learned to live with the accounting maze and to charge Uncle Sam for all the extra books and records. Newcomers to negotiated defense or aerospace contracts are forced to accept the different accounting rules if they want the business. Firms who do most of their business in the commercial market are chased away from selling to Uncle Sam by the accounting confusion; it just isn't worth the hassle.

Buyocracy, however, shows little signs of cleaning up the accounting confusion, despite government's often-stated desire to bring more firms into the market. Each agency is convinced that its accounting regulations are the proper rules and that the other government bodies are too stubborn to change their ways.

DATA RIGHTS

No matter what information the government seeks, it wants it supplied in microscopic detail. Often this includes the innermost secrets and proprietary data of a company. Usually contractors can mark the information "confidential" or "proprietary," and government offices are expected to protect such data as tightly as it guards its own secrets. However, bureaucracy has enough trouble trying to prevent pervasive leaks of government secrets, let alone stopping leaks of company secrets entrusted to Uncle Sam. There is such a constant employment migration from industry to government and back to industry that company proprietary data often does not remain under government lock and key. With so much sharing of data among federal agencies, proprietary notations can become obscured or overlooked.

In some cases, buyers simply ignore or overlook contractor-denoted proprietary labels on data and use it for their own agency advantage. Company proprietary engineering drawings supplied to a program office may suddenly become part of a new competitive bid package. A major instrument firm took twelve years to prosecute a patent infringement claim against the Air Force, which had turned the entire data package for a patented oscilloscope over to competitors.

There is a risk that rivals can unearth private company data stored in agency files through Freedom of Information cases. Confidential material may be publicly exposed through subpoenas by government agencies, Congressional committees, or the courts.

Strategy: Honor all government requests for data—you can usually do nothing else—but keep a trick up your sleeve. There is often some art, some fine tuning, that does not show on engineering drawings but is essential in producing an item. Supply all the drawings if you must, but keep hold of the necessary magic to make the drawings work. Demand to be paid for data packages given the government. Too often Uncle Sam ends up with a gold mine of proprietary data that came through the paperwork mill.

Frequently, agencies and contractors end up in a negotiation standoff over company proprietary information. It is to the government's interest to get as much data as possible without strings. Then it can use the material as it sees fit—for new procurements, as a yardstick to assess competitors, or as a guideline to standards and governmentwide specifications. Contractors, of course, want to keep as much data secret as possible to lock up future procurements for themselves and to control present programs that they have with the government.

The distinction between company proprietary data and government data becomes blurred on projects in which both parties have invested. An agency pays to modify a firm's commercial off-the-shelf product. The government has data rights to all the modifications it funds, but the company still wants to protect its basic proprietary product. The question of who owns what in such an arrangement can provide enough court work to keep lawyers on both sides occupied for years. Happily, data rights can be allocated through compromise on most government projects, but a company must stand firm for its rights in all negotiations. It may be as crucial to a firm's success to retain rights to any data as it is to negotiate a good contract.

There is another side to data rights which contractors don't bring up: industry's unabashed appropriation of government data to make products for the commercial market. Not infrequently, contractors build on government drawings for a modified product that they then patent for themselves.

This paperwork does not throw smart contractors. They learn how to work the system to keep the paper tiger from biting.

15
AUDITS
"You Oughta Done Differently"

- THE WHO, WHAT, WHERE, WHEN, AND HOW OF AUDITS

- WHEN YOU ARE EXEMPT

- STANDING UP FOR YOUR RIGHTS

15. AUDITS
"You Oughta Done Differently"

A Navy booklet for prospective bidders happily talks about the "partnership of the Navy and industry working closely together in the nation's interest."

Some partnership. The first contact the Navy's new contractor is likely to have with its "close partner" is a plant visit by hordes of Navy auditors. They will pry through the books, snoop through the plant, and query the firm's banker on minute details of all its operations. This can be followed by Defense Contract Auditing Agency probers, covering much the same ground. Then can come auditors from the General Accounting Office, Internal Revenue Service, Securities and Exchange Commission, Federal Trade Commission, Justice Department, Equal Employment Opportunities Office, and Occupational Safety and Health Administration.

Labor Department examiners will scour the firm's wage rates and can even dictate what it will pay if the firm is a service contractor to the government. (See Chapter 19, "At Your Service: A $20 Billion Business.") If the company uses imported components, it may face U.S. Customs Service auditors. If it exports, it may run afoul of Commerce Department Export Control Office auditors. Even after running the gauntlet of these probers, the firm may yet face the Renegotiation Board auditors years after the contract has been finished.

No one knows for sure just how many auditors Uncle Sam has throughout the bureaucracy. As expected, IRS has the most, about 14,000. The Defense Contract Audit Agency (DCAA) has 3300 to 3500 at any one time. GAO has 4000 auditors. However large the auditor census is, there are enough federal gumshoes to pry into every part of a contractor's business.

Certainly federal agencies must check company performance. There is no guarantee of sainthood in industry, and government would be remiss in not monitoring observance of rules. One audit uncovered a massive $29 million cost overrun in a key Department of Defense communication program not previously revealed by the firm. However, federal auditors rarely win any popularity contests. No firm likes to be stripped naked with possible demands for extra payments of hundreds of thousands of dollars.

Auditing can start even before a firm wins the contract. If the company is not well known to the program office—and on large programs, even if it is—a preaward audit of the firm's financial status and ability to perform is usually made. Often this is the first hint a bidder has that it is in a strong position to win.

> *Caution:* The auditors' appetite is insatiable, but a prea-
> ward audit does not give them license to run amok through
> every corporate document or financial record. If auditors are
> seeking data not germane to the bid, the company can re-
> fuse to produce such records. This could be a factor in any
> eventual negotiations, since the auditor will report such re-
> fusal to the project contracting office. The auditors may also
> be part of the government negotiating team, making refusal
> even stickier. When in doubt, check a good government
> contract lawyer; this may save you grief in the end. Courts
> have also ruled that clauses in contracts giving GAO the
> right to examine company documents directly related to the
> contract are not an "open Sesame" for GAO to rummage
> through all company books.

To understand government auditors, companies must know:

Auditors Get Good Marks by Uncovering Skeletons in the Contractor's Closet. Government contracting is so complicated, bookkeeping requirements are so confusing, directives so vague, that auditors can usually spot something. Ambitious auditors may scour your records until they do find something, no matter how minor.

Corporate tempers are thin during the ordeal of audits, which may go on for days or even weeks. The temptation often is to snap back at the object of hostility at hand—the auditors. But if probers have managed to come up with only minor infractions, consider yourself lucky. The audit probably cost Uncle Sam a hundred times more than what the small infraction that was uncovered was worth, and time lost from company operations probably cost an equal amount. But auditors are searching for "what might have been." Be glad they didn't find it in your operation.

The government is not totally ignorant of the high cost of auditing when little return can be expected. A few years ago the Department of Defense finally got wise and dropped audits on orders for less than $10,000, figuring any money errors caught would never equal the expense of the audit.

Some agencies, particularly the Department of Defense, have tried to cut down continual and costly audits by making a one-time, intensive inspection of whatever part of a vendor's operation is being monitored, whether it is the management plan, manufacturing quality control, or fiscal controls. The agency will then certify the firm's operation in that area, eliminating repeated audits in the future except for spot checks. Sounds good in theory; in practice, however, bureaucracy just can't break the habit of sending in auditors, even when a firm's operation has been given Uncle Sam's seal of approval. GAO once chastised the Air Force for keeping sixteen procurement analysts working full time at a major aerospace plant, even when Air Force headquarters had previously approved the firm's management system.

The Department of Defense (DOD) also gives some contractors a partial break on auditing through a program with the confusing name, "Contractor Average Weighted Share," which exempts firms predominately in the commercial market from audits of company overhead and indirect costs. The reasoning is that the highly competitive fixed-price commercial market will force down company overhead costs to reasonable levels. The real reason is probably a shortage of DOD auditors. Monitors freed from surveying companies that are largely commercial can be used to scrutinize defense contractors, which charge almost all their overhead costs to Uncle Sam. If you sell mostly to the commercial market, be sure you are included in the relaxed auditing provisions of Contractor Average Weighted Share. At this writing, you qualify if 75 percent of your total company sales are to the commercial market or in fixed-price government contracts. (DOD believes the same internal pressure to cut overhead expense motivates firms on fixed-price contracts also.)

Everybody Gets into the Auditing Act. The program manager can call on the agency's own probers to examine a company's financial and performance records. A separate contract administrator within the program office can call out the same troops, as can higher agency superiors. The agency often has its own resident inspector located right in the contractor's plant if the job is big enough. While resident inspectors usually have no authority to go ferreting through company books, they can demand a wide range of cost and production documents related to work being performed. The Defense Contract Audit Agency routinely checks each contract, and we have seen the army of other probers that can get involved in the same contract.

All too often, this results in the lowest-common-denominator approach to auditing. A company can keep getting a clean bill of health from each group of auditors until one set spots a suspected error. A firm may feel it is home free after the in-plant inspector, program office reviewers, and contract officer find nothing wrong— only to have DCAA or General Service Administration auditors question some transactions.

In the worst cases, contractors may actually think they are following instructions of in-plant inspectors, only to have subsequent auditors disapprove of the very recommended action.

A vendor may feel that a contract cost problem is solved when the contract officer signs the change. After all, the contracting officer is the government's legal authority on a contract. But a string of auditors can later overturn that contracting officer's decision— sometimes years later. A remodeling firm was told by its contracting officer that it did not have to replace thermostats in refurbishing Army family housing units. The agency inspector said nothing. A year later an auditor claimed that everyone had erred and that ambiguous contract specifications did require the thermostats to be replaced, which the unlucky firm was forced to do.

The Customer Is Always Right in Audit Disputes. Government regulations are so complex, data and records required so massive, that many audit findings turn on minor legal interpretations. A firm changed a subcontractor midway through the project but did not report a $74,000 cost savings. The firm was zapped later by auditors, who cited directives requiring even a vendor with a fixed-price contract to report such lower cost subcontracts. Another firm charged off a one-day plant closing for the funeral of the owner as a direct labor cost, but eagle-eyed auditors would not allow it. All auditors can cite some regulation, no matter how obscure, to back their findings. If companies want to fight what they consider an unjust decision, they may find that the legal cost exceeds the extra amount they will have to fork over to Uncle Sam.

Contractors Not Only Have to Endure Auditors; They Must Pay for the Privilege. Initially, there is the staggering paperwork cost of the mountain of documents required for government audits. Some of the expense can be charged back to Uncle Sam through administrative overhead rates on government contracts, but most firms doubt that they can fully recoup the spiraling paper cost.

Valuable management time is lost while auditors go through company records with endless questions. If agencies suspect any big trouble, entire auditing squads, termed "tiger teams" in industry jargon, can be called in to spend weeks going through corporate documents and procedures.

Contractors can be kept dangling for months before bureaucrats make a final determination. Often, the first auditors are minor-grade GS-9 and GS-10 civil servants who keep checking back with superiors before making any decision. They do not want to risk being overruled by higher authorities in the agency, but all this takes valuable time. Review of audit reports by program officials gets bogged down—more time lost. Review of reports is further delayed by constant turnover of program staffs, meaning that new persons must become familiar with standing contracts. During this time the company may be making continued command performance briefings before many levels of the agency—paying travel, executive time, and documentation expenses out of its own funds.

Know Your Agency. One agency may be an auditing terror, while another rarely looks at reports even if it asks for them. GAO found that the Veterans Administration had processed only two cases of negligence on the part of architects in thirty years.

Even offices within a single agency are not consistent. One office hardly looks at auditor reports; another office in the same headquarters has auditors working overtime to probe the smallest cost details. Such uneven auditing is hardly fair to vendors. One contractor may be pilloried for alleged shortcomings that the same agency overlooks for its competitors on another project. About the only answer buyocrats give to such dichotomy is that it's government business. Consider it a favor of the gods if a project office turns out to be an auditing patsy.

Agencies do not present a united front on auditing either. Project office managers often resent Monday-morning quarterbacking from auditors just as much as contractors do. Contract officers must often make complicated, high-risk decisions based on their best judgment at the moment. They do not take kindly to auditors second-guessing such decisions months, even years, later. Frequently they will stand behind contractors in the face of adverse auditor reports to defend their own positions.

Unfortunately, auditing reports can become a political hot potato, regardless of their merit. Lawmakers, competitors, or opponents within the bureau itself can leap on an adverse audit or twist it out of context. Thus, project officials tend to take a safe course in contract decisions—or better yet, to take no direction at all, riding both sides of an issue. They fear being outguessed by auditors in some distant future.

Most haggling concerns contractor costs in negotiated awards. Any firm knows the difficulty of figuring costs precisely. Even satisfying internal company auditors on cost allocation can be a major exercise. But federal auditors are masters at second-guessing costs—or, more precisely, how a firm overcharged the government and should have had lower costs.

The irony is that on a majority of negotiated contract bids for DOD and major civilian federal agencies, contenders must document every major cost element of their proposal. Not only that, but firms must certify the costs and reimburse Uncle Sam later if they come up with any lower costs. (See Chapter 14, "Paperwork: How To Keep From Being Buried.")

Before the contract award, auditors are usually all over a firm's proposal to review its cost estimates. With such pervasive probing, one wonders how buy-ins with unrealistic cost estimates (See Chapter 8, "Winning at Any Price") or alleged excess profits on other contracts can occur. A tenet of bureaucracy may be at work here: the more microscopic the probe made on bid proposals, the more details are going to be overlooked.

Once a firm's cost estimates clear the first auditing hurdle, they face continual scrutiny throughout the life of the contract, sometimes even after work has been completed. At any time auditors may disallow costs that a company is charging off against its contract. The project contract officer has the final decision on costs to be allowed, but it takes a courageous official to countermand the auditors. A contractor has thirty to sixty days in most cases to appeal any cost disallowed by auditors to the project contracting officer. If this deadline is missed, the auditors' decision may become final without any action by the contract office. Companies can carry their fight to higher contract administration appeals boards within an agency, but often the legal fees would be more than the disallowed cost.

Bureaucrats also have an auditing court of last resort—the Renegotiation Board.* Since the Korean war, this board has audited aerospace and defense contractor books for possible excess profits, which is defined as higher than normal profits due to crash buying needs. The board can unilaterally determine what excess profits may have been made and order the contractor to repay the government. Companies can appeal to the federal courts. In reality, many amounts are small enough not to warrant the expense of a court fight; companies just pay, even when they feel strongly that they are in the right.

Powers of the Renegotiation Board wax and wane, according to the political climate. Attempts are made to expand coverage to all negotiated government contracts. Industry routinely lobbies to abolish the board. A creature of the Korean war sudden mobilization buildup, the Renegotiation Board survives, as do most bureaucratic relics, because politicians find it easier just to continue an agency than to abolish it.

Unfortunately, small firms and prols most often fall victim to Renegotiation Board findings of excess profits. A ten-year analysis of board records shows that big contractors are nailed in only 15 percent of the cases. The small firms obviously are easier targets than the major contractors with high-paid legal counsel. Small firms also lack subtle techniques for burying excess profits throughout the financial books. Renegotiation auditors have a greater motivation to pick on small firms: they are less likely to fight board decisions and will settle or concede.

Contractors often find the way an audit is conducted more infuriating than the audit itself. There is a very human tendency of many probers to use a heavy hand. Companies that are trying to serve their government often end up feeling they are being treated as common criminals.

In the past, U.S. Customs Service auditors have swooped unannounced into company offices to seize file cabinets of corporate records. Most executives are annoyed that such raid tactics are

---

* Bills were pending in Congress at the time this book went to press to abolish the Renegotiation Board or put it on a standby basis for wartime use only.

necessary. They note that the Internal Revenue Service follows normal examining procedures on tax liabilities that far exceed any disputed tariff payments sought by customs agents.

Federal Trade Commission investigators spent an entire day combing through one firm's records. On leaving the executive offices, the FTC gumshoes dutifully copied the names of all magazines and newspapers on executive desks. Perhaps the government needs to vacuum up every shred of possible information, but disgruntled officials of this firm wondered if Orwell's Big Brother had actually arrived to question even the publications they read.

Federal auditors generally are dedicated, qualified professionals, but some agencies are plagued by high turnover and an inability to attract high-caliber talent. These problem agencies tend to give a bad name to otherwise conscientious federal auditing practices. A persistent problem for all agencies, however, is lack of direction for auditing troops. Agency audit manuals are often hopelessly out of date and many times are vague and confusing. Not enough training is given in rapidly fluctuating procurement rules.

Some agencies are so hard-pressed to recruit auditors that they contract out auditing to private independent firms. There is obviously less agency control with contracted audits. Frequently there is no continuity as contract auditors are changed year after year. GAO complains that many agencies fail to monitor contract auditors, raising the question, "Who audits the auditors?"

There are many records that the government has legal right to examine through tax laws or procurement regulations that are negotiated into a firm's contract, but this does not give auditors the right to conduct unlimited search expeditions. When in doubt, see your lawyer. Stand up for your rights.

Many federal auditors arrive with legal subpoenas, and uninitiated contractors often succumb to such awesome documents. Unfortunately, there is virtually no checkpoint in the vast bureaucracy to stop minor levels of agencies from broadsiding subpoenas and demands for endless records and data. Even the smallest firm should stand up to fight such subpoenas. Many times buyocrats on a tenuous fishing expedition back down quickly when facing such a challenge.

Another temptation of federal auditors is to second-guess company decisions to claim overpayment or excessive costs to the government. The Defense Contract Audit Agency charged that one large firm could have saved $1 million by better production scheduling. A food caterer to government offices was socked for $800,000 by auditors who questioned the firm's procurement methods. Another auditor challenged a firm's using its own corporate plane rather than commercial airlines.

Contractors resent buyocrats telling them how to run every aspect of their business. It is all too easy for an auditor with no other management concerns to second-guess a corporate decision, and often the result is a years-long fight simply to justify business decisions most observers would consider sound.

This does not mean that all contractor practices are beyond challenge. Agencies must make audits to be sure that companies and government contract officers have acted properly. Also, auditors can often do firms a favor by discovering wasteful practices or recommending sound ways to cut costs. Neophyte government contractors could be especially helped by veteran agency auditors in setting up good cost-control systems.

As with other aspects of federal procurement, a balance must be struck in audits. If Uncle Sam doesn't try to play the heavy and vendors don't view every auditor as an interloper and spy, contract review will work as it should—to the benefit of all parties.

·

16
CLAIMS AND OTHER SQUATTER RIGHTS

- TRYING TO MAKE UNCLE SAM PAY THE COSTS WHEN THE AGENCY IS AT FAULT

- TEN COMMANDMENTS FOR PROCESSING CLAIMS

- THE BEST WAY TO RESOLVE CLAIMS FIGHTS: SETTLE OUT OF COURT

16. CLAIMS AND OTHER SQUATTER RIGHTS

Many government contracts end up in dispute or with claims and counterclaims flying between vendors and the customer. A whopping 1900 claims are filed each year on federal contracts. However, high as this seems, it is less than 0.1 percent of all government contracts. The bulk of work for Uncle Sam does not end up in litigation but is performed normally without protest and acrimony.

Still, the odds are good that at some time a contractor will run into a legal snarl with the bureaucracy. That sets the stage for a complex claims process, which may take years to resolve without any clear satisfaction for either party.

Many causes of claims have already been discussed: poor bid specifications, project mind-changing, a complex program that no one can get together, government-furnished equipment arriving late, tight budgets forcing program delays. Contractors file claims to recover damages. The government does likewise.

Even more claims result from government charges against contractors: faulty performance, late delivery, failure to meet any of a hundred boilerplate contract clauses.

No matter which party is at fault, the vendor soon learns that Uncle Sam holds the trump cards in claim cases.

· The program office immediately deducts any money it claims is due, but the contractor must wait months, and usually years, to collect any money on a claim against the government. Contractors must borrow funds to make up the difference or absorb the deficit while hoping someday to recover it from Uncle Sam.

· The government can afford to wait indefinitely on claim cases; most contractors cannot. The pressure is on vendors, especially prols and cash-tight small companies, to settle quickly for almost any sum to which the program office will agree.

· Bureaucrats will always prefer year-long claims litigation to admitting a mistake and accepting a contractor's claim immediately. To confess to a costly error could be a black mark on an official's career record, but officials lose little in claims cases and gain extra time to dig out of the program hole. At the very least, the long delays cover their tracks, and even if the program office loses a case, the official may be transferred elsewhere or the agency will have forgotten the details.

• Agencies can count on an army of government lawyers, auditors, and technicians to fight their legal case. Vendors, particularly small firms, have only limited legal counsel. Buyocrats have resources through exhaustive audits to probe the most minute details of a company's financial records. The contractor has virtually no access to government records and may have to go to court through Freedom of Information suits to pry loose the few documents it does get.

• Sometimes a contractor is sent on a round-robin as one agency sends the claim to another agency. This happens all too often when more than one federal office is involved. If the General Services Administration is handling negotiations for another agency's procurement, each may tell the unlucky vendor to file with the other's board of claims. The Pentagon often buys some specialized products for civilian agencies and again a contractor may have trouble getting either agency to handle its claim.

• Contract terms and conditions can be so ambiguous that they deny a vendor any grounds for a claim, like the Army base officers' club that terminated the booking agent's contract to provide entertainment over a dispute on the quality of rock-and-roll bands procured, or the painting contractor who locked horns with the Army over the exact tone of a color for a barracks project.

• So many agency officials may get in the act that an aggrieved contractor has trouble knowing who is the real power on the case. True, only the contracting officer on the project can make any legal decisions on claims, but often the C.O. only fronts for a multitude of agency officials with a hand in the claims case. More than one executive in the project office may communicate with the contractor, all under the name of the single legal contracting officer. Often there is very little real "negotiation" to try to settle a claim before it goes into litigation because the contracting officer has been given a predetermined position by superiors which the officer cannot change.

Despite such a one-sided setup, agencies do lose claim cases to clever contractors. Program offices frequently keep poor records, and a well-documented vendor can take advantage of this to win its case. Buyocrats often are merely trying to cover up their own glaring mistakes, which courts or higher agency claims boards will not allow. Agencies often so mismanage a program that even if the vendor is at fault, it can get higher authorities to sustain claims against inept officials.

Success in claims cases comes from knowing how to play the game. There are definite rules and strategies, and, surprisingly, some of the biggest contractors often overlook them.

Every government contract should have a disputes and claims clause among the terms and conditions. Usually it is a boilerplate clause simply stapled among the mass of other duplicated standard legal clauses. Because of this, the dispute clause is frequently overlooked or reviewed hastily by even experienced contractors, although its wording sets the precise ground rules for filing any future claims under the pact. This clause can mean hundreds of thousands of dollars to the contractor—the difference between a profit or loss on the contract.

Most dispute clauses will set a deadline, frequently thirty days, for filing a claim. Vendors should be sure they can live with the deadline; otherwise, a late claim will be automatically thrown out.

Watch: Agencies often try to get claims thrown out for being late by citing some ambiguous oral decision of the project office months before. Claims appeals boards generally start the deadline clock running only after a written decision, and contractors should insist on this deadline.

Watch: Another popular ploy of government contract officers is to drag their feet or simply refuse to make a decision on a disputed contract matter. This leaves the contractor hanging, since appeals boards consistently refuse to take cases until there is a contracting officer decision to appeal. A deliberate stall can sometimes make a prol or a desperate firm back down on its original claim just to get some limited concession from the project office. Once the contracting officer makes a decision, no matter how tardy, the vendor can claim extra damages resulting from the stall.

The contractor's first appeal for relief should be to the project office. Initially it may be only a letter, or it may be a hundred-page legal proposal.

1. Whatever the form, *put everything in writing.* Oral petitions can be misinterpreted. They establish no legal record that can be reviewed. In fact, the project office can deny ever receiving the appeal. Address all contract claims and appeals to the contracting officer, who is the person legally responsible for your contract. In-plant inspectors, lower-level program managers, even agency superiors may promise anything orally. Only the contract office, however, has authority to alter your contract. Appeals boards consistently reject claims based on verbal promises from any other government representative. An ammunition shell manufacturer spent $107,000 on extra refinishing of shell casings, based on an oral approval by the in-plant inspector, only to find it could not collect the extra money because the contracting officer had not approved the change.

2. Get the contracting officer's decision *in writing.* The same lack of written record can sabotage a claims appeal when the project office denies any verbal decision allegedly made on a contract. A small contractor thought it had gotten oral agreement for a two-month delay on a construction project, only to find that there was no written evidence supporting its claim when the contract was later terminated for default.

3. Keep copious records on contract performance. Be prepared to document every aspect of a claim. Bureaucracy frequently keeps such bad records itself—or cannot retrieve documents from the mountains of federal paperwork—that a vendor can win an appeal simply on the basis of better records.

4. Contractors with small claims, usually under $25,000, may be able to get quicker nonhearing decisions from agency contract appeals boards. Many times, such small cases are decided within thirty days, so firms are spared year-long waiting to recover possible claims. Two-thirds of all claims with federal agencies fall into this

class. On these claims small-firm executives may represent themselves. After all, they have lived with the problems intimately and are probably as well prepared as anyone to press the case.

5. If the stakes are even moderately high, consider getting specialized legal help. Claims attorneys are not cheap; frequently the claim is so small or prospects for full recovery are so thin that it's just not worth the cost. One firm spent $3350 on legal fees to fight a claim and ultimately got $450 from the government. However, if a claim is important, a claims attorney is probably needed. Presidents of small firms often try to argue their own claims before contract officers and claims boards but prove no match for the legal arsenal that agencies can command. Many executives feel their claim is so just that it will be accepted by a claims board. They are surprised to learn of the amazing legal agility of buyocrats, obscuring data and sidetracking issues.

6. Be sure to take the right legal action. One firm sought $57,000 in extra costs from a contract termination under the disputes clause of the pact. After three years of litigation, the agency contract appeals board rejected the claim because it said action should have been filed under the contract's termination clause. The unfortunate vendor pointed out that it was now far past the one-year deadline to file claims under the termination clause, but the claims board said, "Tough luck; we can't rewrite contracts."

7. Be sure you can wait out a long claims litigation. If the contracting officer will not agree to a claim, the vendor can take the case to the agency board of contract appeals and ultimately to the federal courts. Even the Pentagon appeals board expressed dismay at one claims case still going on after nine years. Many prols and small firms cannot afford to wait for the government in hopes of collecting large claims and are forced to settle for only a fraction of the money in dispute. Uncle Sam does now pay interest on any claims starting from the date of the contract action, but this small interest often

is not enough to offset the high delay costs for a small firm.

Even the largest primes get zapped by the long claims litigation process. Firms with claims running into the tens of millions of dollars must borrow these funds until they collect from Uncle Sam. In times of tight cash flow, waiting for appeals boards or courts to rule on big claims causes plenty of front-office consternation.

8. Claims fights can be dirty. One contractor had a key official resign, and the official was later called as a government witness. Agencies can call your competitors to testify on "normal industry practices" that allegedly refute your claim.

9. Everybody can quote government regulations to back their cases. Many claims disputes boil down to a "my regulation" versus "your regulation" shootout between contractor and government. Unfortunately, when the government is both judge and defendant, the buyer's legal interpretation often wins out. An air transportation charter service was ordered to return $600,000 on a charter contract with the Air Force when the federal excise tax on fuel was lowered. The carrier argued that its rates were set by the Civil Aeronautics Board and it could lose its license if it discriminated on lower rates to one customer over another. No matter. The Pentagon Contract Appeals Board ruled that the standard tax rebate clause in the contract forced the carrier to refund the money, regardless of the CAB regulation.

10. Be careful on all releases signed at the conclusion of a contract. Most releases signed at the time of final payment allow a vendor to submit claims for some specified period later, usually about five to six years after the end of the contract, but some buyers get unwary firms to sign absolute releases at the end of a contract, barring any later claims. Should such a contractor later discover a fault against the government, it has no recourse for action; it has signed away its rights.

Only prime contractors can press claims against the government. What about subcontractors who may have a dispute with

Uncle Sam? A key subcontractor on a Navy ship gunfire control system ran up $458,000 in extra costs when the Navy was four months late supplying a critically needed radar system. A large sub on an Air Force fighter plane was ordered to refund $729,000 for alleged overpricing on components. Both subcontractors had to convince the prime contractor to file their claims for them, since the government's contracts were legally with the primes.

This can be risky. Primes may not fight as aggressively for the rights of subcontractors as when their own company interest is at stake. Primes may allow the subcontractor's lawyers to stand in on the case, but this requires extra time and coordination. If the prime does not want to upset its own good standing with the agency, it may make a lukewarm appeal at best for the sub.

Some contractors suddenly find themselves saddled unexpectedly with claims cases acquired by the merger with another firm. Often the legal time to research such acquired claims exceeds any possible return from Uncle Sam.

Sometimes, even when claims are upheld, contractors get only partial victory. Disgruntled agencies can hold up claims payments for months for many petty reasons. One project office refused to pay the claim until a construction contractor got the approval of its bondsman, even though construction had been completed two years before. It cost the firm an extra $2600 to reprocess the surety approval, just to force the project office to pay funds that were legally its due.

Agencies who lose their case before an appeals board or court can ask for a reconsideration of the decision. That alone delays payment of the claim, and if the buyer is clever enough to find a loophole in the original decision, the ruling may be overturned. Often, if an agency's lower-level staff counsel lost the initial claims case, the top agency legal eagles are assigned to win a reconsideration. Companies also have the right to ask for reconsideration of an adverse decision but have a far poorer batting average in turning rulings around.

Occasionally a company may fight a claim through the agency appeals board for years and have the claim upheld on legal principles, only to have the case referred back to the original contract office to settle the amount to be paid. Often the vendor and buyer lock horns in a second battle over money due, which takes another year to go through the agency claims board.

Some victories are hollow. One construction firm seeking $69,996 in claims was awarded a grand total of $67 for extra concrete reinforcing. Another construction firm won its claim for extra expense for bulldozers to take out rock not shown in the government's ground site plan, which caused an extra month's delay in the work; the Air Force assessed the firm $73,000 for the delay. The astonished contractor went back to the Pentagon appeals board, claiming the delay was the government's fault because of its faulty ground plan, but was rejected because the board held that the firm had settled that claim.

Many claims cases are absurd. A patch manufacturer sought $2700 for making military insignias because it claimed the Army specifications were so faulty that extensive rework had to be done. The Army project office didn't want to admit it had written a bad spec so it fought the claim. The case covered five months of hearings before the Pentagon claims board, requiring 3100 pages of testimony. After all this, the appeals board found both parties at fault and told them to go back and settle their differences.

Veteran industry and government officials all agree: the best way to settle a claim is before it goes into litigation. Often there are no winners in a protracted legal dispute. However, settling disputes in the early stages takes the good will of both parties. Unfortunately, contractors or program officials frequently refuse to budge on any point, almost guaranteeing a long claims battle. The ideal situation is for reason to prevail in a contract dispute so both sides can settle their differences early and avoid needless delay, costs, and hard feelings.

17

TERMINAL ILLNESS
When Your Contract Is Canceled

• **WHAT TO DO WHEN THE CUSTOMER CANCELS A CONTRACT FOR CONVENIENCE**

• **TERMINATION FOR DEFAULT: YOU'RE TO BLAME**
Warning signals: cure notice and show-cause letter
Breaking bad news to the customer
Reprocurement costs: Uncle Sam tags you again

17. TERMINAL ILLNESS
When Your Contract Is Canceled

Contract terminations, like divorce, can be traumatic and expensive and require years of court suits and countersuits. Like a marriage breakup, it can come without warning—a telex out of the blue: "Contract DAAB-0522-77-C-0531 is terminated effective this date. Please cease all work and stop all orders in process." The reasons for such sudden rupture can be obscure, or the breakup can be a long time coming, with plenty of storm clouds and fury. Still, the final contract termination notice is no less painful, no less costly for all the festering buildup.

Basically, there are two broad types of terminations: for convenience of the government or for default by the contractor.

TERMINATION FOR CONVENIENCE OF THE GOVERNMENT

Uncle Sam can stop a contract at any time, for reasons as varied as running out of money on the project to simply not needing the product or service any more. The Army terminated a big order for truck axles six months after it was awarded when an inventory check showed the service had a twenty-year supply of the same axles already on hand. A charter bus company's contract to provide service on an air base was canceled with a year to run when the base commander decided the Air Force could run its own buses at less cost. The Air Force terminated a computer terminal firm's contract after only one month when the service discovered an error in its original RFP.

Some government contracts, particularly those for rental equipment, have a thirty-day cancellation clause with no penalty to Uncle Sam. Under this arrangement, the contracting officer needs only give the vendor a month's notice, and the government can cancel without giving any reason. Many bankers refuse to provide credit for work under contracts with thirty-day cancellation clauses, claiming they are not contracts at all when the government is free to back out on such short notice. But often federal buyers can force such onerous clauses on prols who are afraid not to agree. Vendors in highly competitive fields can be forced by buyocrats into accepting thirty-day cancellation clauses. But the first defense against such risk obviously is to try to stand up to government negotiators and resist signing such clauses. Too many firms ignore boilerplate cancellation clauses or fail to make a strong demand against them. Others delude themselves into thinking agencies will not cancel a contract on such short notice when millions of dollars of sophisticated equipment has been rented. These firms are often surprised when buyocracy orders the gear taken out because the agency has gotten a lower price quotation from a competitor.

Counterploy: Many a vendor has kicked out an incumbent with a thirty-day cancellation contract through an unsolicited proposal with a much lower price than the agency is now paying.

If the government cancels a contract for its own convenience, however, the agency must pay any damages incurred by the vendor. This can become a hassle, even when the government is clearly liable. In the first place, the very contracting officer who terminated the pact becomes the judge and jury on damage claims filed by the firm. Many project offices try to handle claims in a fair and businesslike fashion, and vendors are reimbursed for their damages without too much trauma. However, all too often buyocrats try to recoup their own losses at the expense of the innocent contractor. A project office forced to cancel a contract in a sudden budget crunch frequently tries to challenge, delay, or modify damage claims from the vendor. Many prols and small firms can't afford to wait out a full claims fight and believe they must settle for whatever damages they can get. If the stakes are high, hiring an experienced claims lawyer, although they are expensive, might be wise. If the firm is in the district of a powerful member of Congress (see Chapter 12, " 'I've Been Robbed!': the Art of Protesting"), it might enlist that support.

Most terminations for the convenience of the government come with little warning. Bureaucracy often tries to hide a pending cancellation until the last minute. Sometimes the project office itself has no advance word; a sudden budget cut or switch in agency plans at the top leads to an immediate cancellation. The effect is still to drop a bombshell on the unsuspecting vendor, often at the worst possible time. A contractor may be placing large orders to suppliers, hiring extra workers, or stockpiling material when the project abruptly ends. Each of these high costs can then become longstanding claims if they are not accepted right away by the bureaucracy.

> *Strategy:* Almost the only protection is good intelligence at all levels of the agency to warn of impending contract cancellations. Death rattles precede the demise of many projects, and a smart vendor listens for these early warnings. Unfortunately, many executives ignore the danger signals because they don't want to face the possibility of the contract termination.

> *Strategy:* A few contractors, suspecting an imminent project cancellation, will deliberately rush out orders for material. They then enter a large damage claim when termination comes, even offering to rebuy the now unneeded suppliers from the government at ten cents on the dollar. This course is not for the fainthearted.

TERMINATION FOR DEFAULT: YOU'RE TO BLAME

By far the greatest number of contract terminations are for alleged default by the supplier. In this case, the contractor is forced to absorb most of the extra costs that result from the cancellation and may end up owing the government substantial sums.

Many critics charge that bureaucracy does a disservice, not by wholesale termination of contracts, but by limping along with a derelict contractor who deserves to be terminated. This penalizes vendors who can perform—firms that may have bid honestly in the original procurement, only to lose through a buy-in by a gambling bidder hoping to get bailed out by the government if the firm ran into trouble.

> *Strategy:* Competitors who sense a project is in trouble should push at all levels of the agency to get the contract terminated, in order to open up a new opportunity to bid for the project. Too often, firms just drop all interest in a project once they lose the bid. They should keep an eye on the program in their normal marketing coverage of an agency to learn when a little pressure might terminate a faltering project and open up a new bid.

Reasons for default vary widely. Failure to deliver equipment or services by the contract deadline is the most common ground for default. The project office may claim that equipment does not meet contract specifications. A building contractor finished 70 percent of a remodeling job on Army base housing, only to become embroiled in a dispute with the General Services Administration over plumbing specifications. Work stopped when the two parties could come to no agreement, and GSA finally terminated the nearly completed contract.

Unlike sudden cancellations for the convenience of the government, default terminations usually have plenty of telltale warnings. A flurry of correspondence between the company and the project office is sparked by contract problems. In-plant government inspectors, auditors, or icy visits by agency project officials warn a firm that it stands in danger of default. Most companies play for time, hoping to overcome obstinate problems. At this stage, project officials often go along with even the lowliest prol; after all, buyocrats don't want the embarrassment of having selected a bad contractor.

If the situation does not improve, the government follows a prescribed legal ritual leading to eventual termination. In most cases, the offending firm gets a cure notice, a written demand that the offending vendor correct whatever contract problem exists or the pact will be terminated at a specified time in the future. This is no idle threat. The project office has probably checked informally with other suppliers to see how soon they could step in to fill the contract requirements. The agency then sets a deadline for the delinquent contractor to "cure" the problem, which coincidentally is the time it would take to get deliveries promised by other vendors.

Sometimes the cure notice is called a show-cause letter. As the name implies, this gives the company a certain amount of time, usually fifteen to thirty working days, to prove why the project office should not cancel the contract for default.

Privileged firms rarely get cure notices or show-cause letters; disagreements are worked out quietly in closed-door conferences. Primes with some leverage are also able to sway buyocrats to give them extra time, and frequently more money, to work out problems. Occasionally, though, a cure notice is the only effective threat the agency has to try to force a privileged status contractor to knuckle down, since the firm may have a gun at the head of a desperate project officer.

Unfortunately, prols have no such leverage, and a cure notice or show-cause letter means business. Hundreds of contracts are canceled for default throughout the government every month; there are so many terminations Uncle Sam can't keep an exact tally.

A prol must devote its best effort to meet the demands of a cure notice or at least convince the project officials of its ability to perform with a little relief in extra time and effort. Too many small firms are tired of a bad contract with the government by this time and just want to walk away from what they see is a bad deal. This can be costly and can preclude future, more profitable government business. Any firm would do well to take the cure notice seriously at the highest levels of management.

Unless a deficient firm has failed to perform at all, it can often negotiate a little extra time to work out problems. After all, the project office does not want to admit it made a mistake in awarding the contract, especially if it has previously defended the decision during protests from disgruntled losers. Program officials may also gamble that stringing along with the existing errant contractor may be less of a headache than terminating and having to go through an entirely new competitive bid.

A contractor in trouble often faces a dilemma in warning the government of its difficulties. Usually the agency has a host of inspectors, auditors, and project personnel looking over the contractor's shoulder all the time, so there is no chance to hide any ongoing problems. But the firm may be aware of supply difficulties on critical components, technical troubles that have surfaced only in early lab reports, or unexpected cost overhead increases that have not yet shown up in reports to the government.

The thorny dilemma now is when to break the bad news to the customer. One highly reputable radio builder took the Air Force at its word when the service pleaded with contractors to give an early warning of impending program cost increases. The firm told the Air Force of projected cost growth that would not occur for another year. The Air Force promptly terminated the contract and went to a competitor, which, ironically, ran up even higher cost increases. This was small solace to the terminated contractor, who now vows to juggle cost projections so the bad news leaks out gradually.

Strategy: Get the top buyocrats out on a limb early in the program. Have them convince their bosses that it's clear sailing on the project. Then, if trouble crops up, they must answer for their earlier rosy predictions.

Strategy: Don't hide bad news completely so that project offices first learn of problems through audit reports or in a surprise plant visit. Privileged contractors may be able to survive such disclosures, but other firms may lose all bargaining power with project offices that suddenly must break the bad news to superiors—or worse, to Congress. The gradual approach to uncovering ill tidings works best. There is no guarantee that it will always work; exasperated officials who are fed a diet of projections that get worse and worse may tire of the game and terminate the contract anyway.

Buyocracy is frequently without mercy in terminating problem contracts of prols and many primes. The government does not accept many reasons that seem perfectly legitimate to troubled contractors. Warning about these problems was cited as potential proposal booby traps and negotiating pitfalls in earlier chapters, but the major unacceptable alibis bear repeating here:

- Runaway inflation or materials shortage. The privileged firms have little trouble making this excuse stick, but under the government's double standard, prols and many primes get caught in this squeeze over which they may have little control. Appeals boards and claims courts are bulging with decisions upholding terminations when the contractor could not deliver because of unexpected runaway prices or unforeseen materials shortages. The basic rule is: you live with what you bid.

- The supplier of a critically needed part cannot deliver or ships a faulty part. The government makes most firms responsible for their subcontractors; if suppliers falter, the prime contractor is liable. This is true even when contractors use government-designated sources, as many claims board decisions have proved. Just because an agency may have an approved list of suppliers, or may have even designated a single source of supply, if these subcontractors fail to deliver and the project is stymied, the government will still terminate and hold the prime contractor responsible. Buyocrats frequently make a fast, cursory check of industry in order to be able to claim suppliers did exist when they want to refute supply shortage claims. Of course, they are not trying to place an order and get delivery, but appeals boards often accept the word of project officials on flippant checks of supply.

- Bad specifications or engineering drawings supplied by the government. Often such a defense can be very true, since project offices are notorious for providing ambiguous specs and drawings. But this dispute should be taken up with project officials far earlier in the life of the contract. By the time a sick contract reaches the default stage, companies have a hard time making a bad specs and bad drawing alibi stick. At best, the dispute now bogs down in long litigation before claims boards over interpretations of drawings and specs. One unfortunate vendor lost a termination appeal, even though it claimed that smudges of the engineering drawing obliterated a critical welding designation.

- Loss or illness of key employees. Small firms, even a few medium-sized companies, can find contracts seriously crippled when a key engineering official, construction executive, or even the company president walks off the job or becomes incapacitated. But Uncle Sam rarely lets contractors get off the hook for such reasons. Contract termination is usually heaped on top of the accumulating woes of such a troubled firm. Small firms must have contingency plans to cope with key personnel emergencies, or they should stay clear of federal contracts.

- Acts of nature and major accidents. Project officials usually treat such reasons on a case-by-case basis in judging failure to perform on a contract. Buyers are not usually so hardhearted to refuse relief on genuine unforeseen tragedies. But there is still a wide range of events that are debatable and that often require long litigation to settle. Strikes, plant fires, and vandalism are often questioned. Agencies may argue about floods that affected part of plant but left other production facilities unharmed.

If all else fails, a firm can plead for the project office to terminate for the convenience of the government, where few penalties are assessed against the company. This is a type of plea-bargaining, but it makes sense. A project officer may be willing to get such a clean break without years of claims litigation. The government actions may also be partly at blame in the contract trouble, and buyocrats are happy not to expose their own soiled linen. Sometimes the agency is clearly to blame and is just trying to stick the contractor. The Air Force found itself with a four-year supply of airplane bracket parts and wanted out of an existing bracket contract. When the firm was three days late in delivery, the project office tried to get itself off the hook by terminating for default. The company eventually overturned the default action, but only at great legal expense and a year's litigation.

If nothing works out and termination finally comes, here is what a firm can expect:

- To recover little if any of its own costs involved up to then in the contract. A defaulted contractor may find itself liable for stockpiled material, parts on order, special test equipment, or extra employees hired for the project.

- To pay extra costs to the government. This includes repayment of any advances, material, or payments to the firm or disposal costs of material.

- To pay the difference in price if the government is forced to reprocure the product at a higher cost. This reprocurement cost is potentially the most serious liability of all; it is so damaging that it is considered in more detail below.

- To pay high legal costs involved with fighting the termination and processing claims and counterclaims on money due the firm or demanded by the government. Litigation may take years before a company can collect any funds it is due in a terminated contract. Uncle Sam, however, has the edge: the project office can make sure it gets the money it claims it is due, regardless of any counterclaim by the company, simply by withholding the sum from the last progress payment or settlement offer.

REPROCUREMENT COSTS: UNCLE SAM TAGS YOU AGAIN

Procurement regulations of almost all agencies give them the right to solicit new vendors to supply the product or service involved in the defaulted contract. If the new supplier's price is higher than the price of the terminated contract, the defaulted contractor must pay the difference. Sometimes this can be a whopping amount, occasionally double the price of the original contract.

The defaulted contractor is in the poorest position to protect itself in such reprocurement. The project office often goes sole-source to a supplier that can give the quickest delivery, which frequently is the highest price vendor. Even if a new competitive bid is held, the buyocrat is now under no compulsion to get the lowest price, knowing full well that the defaulted contractor is liable to pay the difference of price in the new contract.

Some reprocurements simply seem unjust. An appliance distributor could not get delivery of electric dryers from its manufacturer to meet delivery dates for an Army family housing project, but the very same manufacturer won the reprocurement bid. Another inequity: While a defaulted firm pays for the higher cost of a repurchase, if the government gets a lower price on rebidding, Uncle Sam just pockets the savings.

The defaulted contractor can file a claim if it feels it was abused by an agency's reprocurement action—that either the repurchase price was excessive or the agency was derelict in rebuying the defaulted product or service. Again, such claims may take a year or more to be decided. The defaulted contractor also carries the stigma of guilt for the canceled contract, which is a poor bargaining position for arguing against alleged reprocurement abuses.

Caution: Watch closely to be sure buyocrats don't increase specifications during reprocurement. Program officers can't try to get a higher capability product at the expense of a defaulted contractor. They must reprocure the same product if the defaulted firm must make up the extra cost.

Reprocurement can become mired in sticky debate. If the government is renting equipment on a terminated contract, for how long a time is the defaulted firm liable for higher rents on a reprocurement? What if the agency terminates a lease contract but reprocures under a purchase agreement? What if the agency gets no takers on a rebid? What if the winning bidder in a reprocurement then goes on to make significant changes in the product or service? If the agency must reprocure a similar product, what constitutes "similar"?

Warning: Buyers of surplus government material can find themselves subject to vastly higher reprocurement costs if they default in removing the material they buy. A contractor that offered $100 for the lumber in an abandoned Air Force hangar failed to remove the structure within the thirty-day contract deadline. The service then hired a demolition crew for $3878 to raze the building and assessed the surplus buyer the extra reprocurement expense.

Finally, don't panic with a default notice. A contractor with a reasonable case should fight the action. If the stakes are high, a good claims lawyer may be worth the expense. Many small firm presidents try to avoid costs by representing themselves or using corporate counsel, but specialists are often needed to fend off defaults. Have courage; buyocracy often keeps poor records or cannot justify confusing decisions made during the course of the contract.

Fight back—the results may be surprising.

18

SMALL BUSINESS
It's a Small, Small Whirl

18. SMALL BUSINESS
It's a Small, Small Whirl

It's a typical "government business opportunities conference" for small business. Some thirty-four newcomers to selling to Uncle Sam are there—a few desperate to get any business, others attracted by big government orders they saw their competitors win, most curious about this highly touted $75-billion-a-year market. The member of Congress from the area is always there to kick off the conference with a salute to the contribution of small business to the nation. Low-level agency procurement managers, one after another, deliver stock talks on how they want to do business with small firms. Every speaker showers small business attendees with literature on how to sell to their particular agency. Some booklets are works of art, but hardly informative. Others are entertaining. Some are so legalistic they would qualify for a graduate law school course. The day ends up with individual, face-to-face conferences between the owners of small businesses and agency procurement representatives. There the newcomer gets more literature, a satchel of forms to fill out— even agency telephone directories and organization charts (as if the novice firm can pick up the phone to call the commanding general or cabinet secretary).

Government continually holds such small business briefings. Indeed, the conferences—sponsored by agencies, the Small Business Administration, members of Congress, trade associations, and local chambers of commerce—may be the primary mechanism for recruiting new bidders on government procurements. The meetings have some value; a complete stranger to government selling at least gets a first look at the field and learns some of the jargon and the party line. But *what is not said* at such rallies is often more vital than all the rhetoric. The omissions, of course, are the problems, headaches, and competitive strategies involved in government selling. No agency representative is going to reveal any blemishes; agencies portray an idealized procurement world for small business that simply does not exist.

Bureaucracy cannot ignore small business; the national political ethic has canonized the image of the small entrepreneur, and for good reason: imaginative small firms, unshackled from rigid policies and costly overheads that afflict many large industry conglomerates, have come up with ingenious solutions in many procurements. Almost every industry giant started as an innovative small firm. The growth of technology can come from the wellsprings of small business as much as from giant corporate research and development budgets.

The sheer number of small businesses in America—9 million companies—dictates that they should get their fair share of government procurement. At this writing, small business contributes 48 percent of the business portion of the nation's gross national product. Some 55 percent of all workers in the private sector are employed by small business.

Agencies are apt to tout these statistics at small business briefings. What they don't mention are the less glowing figures of the struggling role of small business in government procurement. Although small firms contribute 48 percent of the business GNP, they averaged 20 to 25 percent of government procurement spending over the last decade. Even these totals do not tell the full story. Most contracts to small business are concentrated in custodial services, small construction, and highly competitive, low-price component and parts sales. In research and development small business averaged only 3 to 5 percent of federal spending. In each of the last four fiscal years, the five major defense contractors received more funding than all of the small business firms selling to the Department of Defense.

Of course, the little firm is most often the prol in government selling. It suffers the fate of the lowest one on the totem in every facet of procurement. These are the unspoken crosses small business bears, which are never aired at buyocrats' rallies.

The small business practitioner who takes up the rally's call for bidders soon begins to learn from hard experience about the real world. The first shock is the "Don't call us—we'll call you" syndrome. Neophytes fill out endless forms, in triplicate and quadruplicate, to get on agency bidders' lists, assured by the briefing conference that their firms will be added to a magical agency directory to receive bid notices on every upcoming procurement in their field. Newcomers wait for their first bid notices. After six to nine months, the suspicion begins to dawn that their firms' listings are incorrect in the agency master directory. The small business person who tries to track down what went wrong through tiered layers of bureaucracy usually ends up with no more satisfaction than simply filling out new forms to try once again to get on the bidders list. Some new firms are lucky; they do receive invitations to bid after getting on agency lists, but many requests are completely out of their field; others require the small firm to fill out yet more forms in order to get a bid solicitation package. Such bid list bungles tend to overshadow the occasions when the System works as it should and newcomers are notified of upcoming bids. Small businesses must be aware of the hit-or-miss workings of agency bidder lists. If they really want to be certain of getting bid notices, *they cannot sit back and wait.* Newcomers must back up their listing with any agency with dogged marketing efforts on many fronts.

Small firms are often directed to small business procurement representatives on each agency's staff. These specialists are supposed to watch for upcoming agency bids on which small business could have a chance and to alert small companies. The agency small business manager is charged with advising and counseling smaller firms on the many bidding problems. This person is supposed to work with prime contractors to get a larger portion of their work subcontracted to small business and is responsible for helping small firms with procurement protests, claims, and government audits. In spite of such an array of duties, most agency small business offices are staffed by a handful of employees. In 1977 the entire Department of Defense had a 600-person small business office to help little firms. By contrast, the Pentagon had 105 specialists working with one of its largest contractors trying to straighten out a procurement boggle.

No matter how dedicated the agency small-business representatives are, their resources are as small as the firms they are trying to serve. One agency small business manager moaned, "It's like chipping away at Mt. Rushmore with an icepick." Less committed small business staffers simply give up. They fulfill their job description flying around the country to give canned pep talks to small business groups.

Strategy: Know your agency small business manager. Despite the odds against them, shrewd staffers can often weasel through the System to help a little firm. They are alert to agency politics, they know what superior officials may be responsive to a small firm's plight, and they sense the critical moment to take a stand. They also know how to maneuver procurement tradeoffs within the agency—"Let's help this small firm to take off some political heat so you can do what you want on this other bid." Such small business managers may need the firm's help to prepare the case and write up the documentation, but be sure there is a chance of success before going to this expense.

THE SMALL BUSINESS ADMINISTRATION

The Small Business Administration, the government's main advocate for the little firm, stirs up as much controversy as do the procurement problems it is supposed to solve for its clientele. Congressional committees, small business groups, even a few bureaucratic reformers—all note the low estate of small firms in selling to Uncle Sam and challenge SBA's record.

SBA is charged with all the procurement duties that the agency small business officers have, but duplication in this case does not double the force for small business. In most cases, it merely dilutes it. All too often, SBA and agency officers toss procurement hot potatoes back and forth without any action.

SBA routinely answers Congressional critics that its staffs are stretched too thin to be effective. The Department of Agriculture has 80,000 workers to service 3 million farms. The Department of Commerce has 29,000 employees to serve 300,000 large firms. SBA has 4500 workers to help 9 million small firms.

The disparity in bureaucracy proves the low priority Uncle Sam gives to small business, despite the ringing tributes to the glory of the little entrepreneur. It does not follow that increasing the SBA bureaucracy will yield a corresponding benefit to small business. Some of SBA's ongoing problems must be corrected first.

The SBA Bureaucracy Is Hard to Find. SBA is divided up into districts, ten in 1977, with each office covering a grab bag of industries from miniature missile connectors to garbage collectors for federal installations. Well-meaning SBA district officials often have little knowledge of peculiar procurement problems afflicting a small firm in the jungle of government selling. They refer the troubled small contractor up or down the SBA bureaucracy or to other government agencies, starting a round-robin of referrals through the bureaucratic maze. One small contractor was shunted from the SBA district office to four different SBA officials in Washington, to the Department of Defense Small Business Assistance Office, to the Air Force Small Business Opportunities Office, to the Hanscom Air Force Base Small Business Procurement Specialist, and finally back to the original SBA district office.

Personal visits are essential. Correspondence gets sidetracked on staff desks or often gets a perfunctory, but unhelpful, reply. Once small business practitioners have traveled the SBA gamut and sized up all officials contacted, they may end up with the names of a few who can be phoned personally on the next problem case. Of course, agency reorganizations and turnover are so frequent that a completely new cast of officials could well be on the scene.

SBA Is Low in the Bureaucratic Pecking Order. No matter how well-meaning SBA officials are, they have little clout. The agency has few legal clubs to hold over other agencies, and good bureaucrats can devise loopholes to escape these SBA edicts. In confrontations with other agencies, SBA must rely on persuasion, conniving, or politicking to work its will. Results depend solely on the bureaucratic finesse of an SBA staffer, not on the merits of the case.

Procurement Overwhelms SBA, Just as It Does Small Businesspeople. Local SBA staffers at major agency buying centers are supposed to watch for upcoming opportunities for small firms to bid, but no SBA representative—no army of SBAers—can possibly track the thousands of wide-ranging programs at even one agency procurement office. A smart SBA local agent will concentrate on a few procurement areas with the highest potential for small business. That doesn't help small firms in fields that can't be watched, but at least a few small contractors may get some leads on upcoming bids. All too often, agency officials throw a few procurement scraps to the local SBA office—token bids that larger firms may ignore anyway. Some agency project officials may want to shut out small firms, for all the anticompetitive reasons explained previously, and they simply hide the upcoming bid from SBA view.

> *Strategy:* A sharp local SBA staffer may not be able to track all pending agency procurements but may go to bat for a small firm to try to stop a sole source or rigged bid, if

alerted. Again, the affected small business practitioner must do the spadework, but having an SBA agent who can run with the ball may turn around an otherwise hopeless cause. Forget it if the local SBAer is merely a correspondence-forwarder.

Caution: Double-check SBA advice on procurements. SBA interpretations or explanations of agency bid packages are not binding; only the word of the specified agency contracting officer has any legal weight. SBA is the closest contact for many newcomers to government business, and these small businesspeople rely completely on what SBA says on a particular bid. Later they find out that their proposals have been rejected because bid requirements were changed from SBA's initial input or because SBA misinterpreted bid specs. Even worse, a small firm may win and think it is signing one contract as outlined by SBA, when actually it has committed itself to something else. Such slipups from SBA are not common, but small firms should be aware that SBA bid and contract interpretations, even though they are made as carefully as possible, are not sacred.

SBA Has a Spotty Record on Promoting Small Business Set-Aside Procurements. The set-aside has long been used in government bids to give small firms a better break. Bids are restricted solely to small business contractors. Tradition rather than any legal basis governs small business set-asides. It is left strictly up to each federal agency to determine how many—and what—bids should be set aside for small business. Historically, less than 5 percent of contract funding is restricted in small business set-asides, mostly in custodial contracts, for mundane, low-price products, or low-profit work shunned by larger firms. Understandably, big firms will fight to block any small business set-asides on contracts these companies are eyeing. Few buyocrats see much purpose in a set-aside confrontation with big business, especially with firms that have strong political clout. So set-asides gravitate toward contracts that nobody else wants.

Agencies compromise by splitting up big procurements, allowing anyone to bid on a portion and restricting the rest of the bid to small business. Called partial small business set-asides, such bids have a tricky wrinkle. If a small firm is low bidder for both parts of the bid, it wins the entire award. If a large firm wins the bid portion open to all comers, the low price on the small business set-aside must be within 120 percent of the large firm's bid price. The low-price set-aside winner then has the option of contracting for the set-aside portion *at the same price* that the large firm bid. The small firm can refuse, and the next low-price set-aside bidder gets the same option if its price was also within 120 percent of the large firm's price. If no small firm accepts, or if all prices on the set-aside portion are above 120 percent of the large firm's price, the big business winner gets the entire award. Complicated? You bet—especially when either the big or the small firm is playing buy-in or fake-out strategy.

> *Strategy:* No one can force agency contract offices to make small business set-asides, but small contractors may be able to work with resident SBA representatives to shame, cajole, lobby, or otherwise connive to increase the number of set-aside bids. Throw in a little political pressure and let it simmer while agencies ponder whether they may be reprimanded. If SBA is ineffective, go directly to key members of Congress to apply set-aside pressure. One small firm, which was in a rare privileged position as favored contractor, conspired with the agency to get locked in through a small business set-aside. No other small firm could qualify and big business was locked out.

The real battle on set-asides may not take place during the bid itself, but over the question of whether a firm is a small business or not. SBA sets various size standards—usually number of employees or annual gross sales volume, depending on the type of industry. That seems clear-cut, except when a firm qualifies as a small business at the time it bids but passes the threshold by the time the contract is awarded, or when a small firm subcontracts out most of the set-aside work to a large business. Size standards are also confused when a large firm has a large equity in the winning small firm of a set-aside bid, when SBA changes the size standards while a bid is in process, or when a firm spins off part of the company to reduce its size to qualify for a small business set-aside. The SBA has a Small Business Size Standards Appeals Board to judge such disputes, and GAO, claims boards, and the courts generally have deferred to SBA decisions in size disputes. It is one of the few procurement areas where SBA reigns supreme, but it wins the agency few fans. Size Standards Appeals Board decisions are often as unpopular with small firms as they are with large ones. Small firm contenders are just as eager as larger compatriots to see a small firm set-aside winner disqualified. Complex interlocking corporate ownerships also lead to convoluted SBA size logic. The board probably is untangling the ownership knots as best it can, but that hardly satisfies opponents to the decision.

There are a few procurement areas in which SBA does reign supreme. Small business sales to Uncle Sam often depend directly on how well SBA is able to enforce its power in the following limited spheres.

CERTIFICATES OF COMPETENCE—COMPETENT JUDGE?

Few project offices want to run the risk of awarding contracts to unknown suppliers that may bomb out. Only the dedicated buy-the-low-price buyocrat, who probably will be shifted to a new job before the bargain-basement contract falls apart, willingly selects the prol. As we've seen, knowledgeable project offices have countless tactics to weed out high-risk bidders, which include mostly small firms. When all else fails, project officials must resort to simply challenging the competence of the small firm to fulfill the contract. If the buyer doesn't challenge the small company's competence, a disgruntled losing contender can. In either case, SBA is the only government agency legally responsible for certifying the small firm as competent. Critics lament that SBA is hardly an impartial judge and that SBA certificates of competence are almost automatic for small firms. This ignores the scores of challenges that SBA upholds, refusing to certify questionable small firms. But as one agency contracting officer says, "A company has to be walking into bankruptcy court before SBA will refuse to certify it as competent." (In one procurement SBA actually did certify a bankrupt firm as competent.)

An agency contract office must award a pact to a selected small business winner once it has been certified as competent by SBA. To get around this mandate, agencies may charge that a small firm doesn't have the "tenacity and perseverance" to complete a contract. To some this may sound like a play on words, but since a small firm's competence is not being challenged, SBA has no legal standing. This tactic has a hidden boomerang: usually, the tenacity and perseverance of only established small contractors can be challenged, since newcomers to government selling have no track record to question. This often eliminates little firms that are committed to the government market, but complete unknowns end up getting awards. Various legislative attempts have been made to allow SBA to rule on any type of challenge to a small business contract award. All have failed up to now. The issue is not easily solved. Procuring agencies must be able to protect themselves against a totally unqualified vendor simply buying into a contract because it has nothing to lose. On the other hand, arbitrarily rejecting small firms kills competition, destroys confidence in the bidding process, and reduces innovative ideas.

MINORITY VIEW ON PROCUREMENT

Government policy is to support minority-owned companies by trying to give them a break in federal procurement. The main way is through a special SBA program called "Section 8(a) programs," after the section of the law expanding SBA authority. This allows SBA itself to act as the prime contractor in any federal program and in turn to subcontract the work to a minority-owned business. The theory is that federal agencies would be more prone to let minority firms do the work if SBA, another part of the government, is legally responsible on the contract. With its neck on the line, SBA also works closely with its Section 8(a) minority subcontractor in management and financial assistance to be sure the contract is fulfilled.

Section 8(a) complaints come less from federal agencies, who seem relatively satisfied with the work being done, than from minority firms themselves and other small businesses. Minority-owned companies charge that the amount of funding is so small that only a small fraction of eligible firms get any subcontracts. In 1977 only forty-four firms in the entire country were sharing in $17 million worth of Section 8(a) contracts. Other small firms complain that SBA merely diverts scarce funds from other programs for Section 8(a), robbing them of needed assistance. As soon as any Section 8(a) subcontractor is judged able to stand on its own feet, the firm is supposed to be moved off the special assistance program, but critics charge that SBA tends to keep the same Section 8(a) subcontractors year after year, preventing new minority subcontractors from getting into the program.

Whatever its faults, however, Section 8(a) offers the best hope for minority small business to get a helping hand from Uncle Sam. Federal agencies themselves are directed to promote contracts to minority firms wherever possible, but such preference must compete with all the other socioeconomic goals federal procurement is supposed to meet (labor surplus areas, assistance to the handicapped, environment, energy conservation). The surest way to success for minority-owned firms is skilled marketing to federal customers, mixing it up with all other contenders. One profitable black contractor in Baltimore sums it up: "The best way to make it is on your own."

Small may not be all beautiful in federal procurement, but small companies may have as good—or better—opportunities to sell to Uncle Sam as they do in the commercial market. It all depends on how they play it.

19

AT YOUR SERVICE
A $20 Billion Business

• WINNING SERVICE CONTRACTS: PRICE, PRICE, PRICE

• REPLACING INCUMBENT CONTRACTORS: EXPECT THE WORST

• WORKING ALL ANGLES TO LINE UP FUTURE BUSINESS

• YOUR BIGGEST COMPETITOR: UNCLE SAM

19. AT YOUR SERVICE
A $20 Billion Business

José Martinez runs a janitorial service with two employees out of a private office in his garage, grossing $78,000 a year. IBM Corporation runs a $16-billion-a-year operation with 250,000 employees around the world. Both have one thing in common: they are government service contractors, following the same procurement rules, coping with the same mountains of paperwork, subject to seeing their federal service contract canceled at any time and awarded to a competitor at 10 percent lower price. Service support business may be the only time a prol like José faces problems similar to those of the industry giants. In fact, he may be better off in this cutthroat field of selling to Uncle Sam.

Government service support work runs the gamut from operating missile test ranges down to running a hot dog stand in the local federal office building. There are so many service support contracts in so many areas for such a variety of federal users that no one knows for sure just how big the market is. The House Government Operations Committee once estimated federal service contracts as a $20-billion-a-year business. Industry officials say that is probably only a minimum figure.

The General Services Administration, the military services, and many other federal agencies hire armies of custodial services, food services, transportation services, clerical assistance, and maintenance help of all types. The U.S. government owns more computers than any other organization in the world, yet Uncle Sam still buys more outside computer service than anyone else. The military services operate their own aircraft repair depots (yes, the biggest anywhere) and still buy more maintenance service from outside firms than all the world's airlines combined.

Service support is probably one of the easiest ways to get into government business. It requires no factory and a minimum of equipment on many projects (and on some projects Uncle Sam supplies much of the equipment). Many times, as we shall see, it requires a minimum number of employees to win a contract—you simply hire the workers away from the former support contractor after you've won the project from it.

Because support work generally does not require massive investments, it is a ball game in which prols and small firms play effectively. Some service contracts are so small that they don't attract larger competitors at all; some of these are janitorial work, fleet car maintenance, and base housing pest control.

Not surprisingly, then, razor-keen competition abounds. Rivals appear out of the ether to contend on service bids. A quick way for former government workers to start their own businesses is to sell their old bosses a service contract. Established service firms often fight back with the only weapon at hand—slashing prices to keep the job. Buyers, knowing a good deal when they have such a market, abet the competitive bludgeoning.

Service support contracts follow the same bid cycle as hardware and product procurements. They fall prey to the same pitfalls and evils as any other government bid. Incumbent vendors and company insiders try to head off bids with sole-source awards or, failing that, to wire in bids for themselves. Service support bids are subject to the same program delays, stretchouts, false starts, stop-and-go funding, changes, cutbacks, and cancellations as other procurements. The same multitude of special contract terms and conditions, inspections, audits, claims, massive documentation, and reports apply.

In addition, government support work has a few wrinkles all its own.

Price Rules Supreme. In most cases, it is the only difference between contending firms. Unlike hardware bids, support contract bidders don't have a better mousetrap they are trying to sell. Generally, the work they must do is precisely spelled out; the only way to set themselves apart from the pack of other bidders is price.

But service contractors have fewer places to cut costs. Support work tends to be highly labor-intensive; yet, labor costs are one of the most expensive parts of any project. The contract may specify the precise number of work hours needed so a service firm cannot cut back on the number of workers to curb payroll costs.

Some support firms cut price by paying lower wages for the same types of jobs than competitors. But labor unions, political pressure, and government regulations increasingly block this practice. The 1965 Contract Service Employees Act requires all government support contractors to pay the "prevailing wage" in a locality for most job categories. Congress has twice expanded coverage to more categories of blue- and white-collar service workers, so the overwhelming bulk of employees must be paid the prevailing wage rate of a given local area. The U.S. Labor Department determines the prevailing wage rate, a process fraught with red tape, delays, and misinterpretations.

Another ploy to cut labor costs is to hire less experienced workers but give them a bigger title. The Navy reviewed a five-year history of one support contract in antisubmarine warfare and found technicians were now being hired to do work formerly handled by Ph.D. engineers.

To Staff a New Support Contract, Hire the Incumbent Firm's Workers. After all, these are the people who know the work better than anyone. Most workers shift to the new contractor rather than lose their jobs. One missile range instrumentation engineer performed the same job for three different firms in five years, going on the payroll of each new contractor as it replaced the incumbent.

> *Caution:* Some newcomers to a service support project fail to hire away key employees of the incumbent firm when they win. They are forced to rush in inexperienced personnel with far higher training expense, greater chance for errors, and possible program slippage. Smart bidders are sure they have enough key personnel already on the payroll to handle any new support contract.

Expect the Worst when You Replace an Incumbent Service Contractor. One service firm performed no routine maintenance of equipment for seven months before another contractor took over. Result: The new firm walked into a mess with frequent equipment breakdowns, high spare parts costs, and much greater maintenance expense than it had counted on. Don't expect the customer to give you any sympathy or extra money—as this firm found out. You get what you bid, but in many cases you get more trouble than you bargained for. Often there is no way to find out beforehand the condition of the equipment the former contractor is leaving you. Frequently the necessary engineering drawings, documents, and manuals turned over to you are incomplete, ambiguous, or out of date. You may be able to press a claim for such inadequacies, but litigation may take years before you can recoup the extra cost.

Caution: Visit the work site, if possible, before preparing your bid. One janitorial service figured floor cleaning was floor cleaning and neglected to inspect the work location. When it won the contract, it found deplorable wax buildup, which the General Services Administration insisted be removed. The unwary firm not only lost its profit, but its workers quit in a huff when forced to scrub the floors on hands and knees with steel wool.

Don't Assume that the Customer Will Let You Phase in Service Work when Replacing an Incumbent. Get such a phase-in written into the contract. A small firm may need time to train inexperienced workers, even in a custodial care contract.

Service Contract Bidders Must Scrutinize RFP Terms, Definitions, and Work Statements. Even experienced contractors can misinterpret RFP statements. One firm ended up with a five-year legal dispute over the definition of the job category of "specialists" required in a service contract, which meant a $10,200 difference in the wage scale the company was forced to pay. A food catering service saw its costs shoot up because GSA insisted that the contract called for higher grade meat.

New Service Contractors Often Replace the Original Equipment Manufacturer. OEM was supporting its own equipment and can be underbid for support contracts because they frequently price service work high to recoup losses they sustained in a highly competitive bid to sell the equipment in the first place.

Caution: OEM firms can shackle competing service contractors by slow delivery of spare parts, by charging excessive prices for critically needed components, or by refusing to supply software or technical details for alleged proprietary reasons.

Agencies Are Even More Unpredictable in Evaluating Service Contract Bids than Hardware Procurements. There are no tires to kick, no products to try out in evaluating proposals. Service contractors are often simply selling their brains—but how do you rate one firm's brain over another's?

Agency evaluations tend to be very subjective. Some contract offices draw up elaborate proposal ranking schemes with a hodgepodge of point values assigned to various parts of the bid. Often any combination of points can be assigned to any contender, depending on the prejudices of the evaluating team. Price is often the only tangible basis for picking a winner, but this may only turn the bid into a lying contest.

Good intelligence inside the agency contract office is even more essential on service support bids—to know if buyers already have a favored firm in mind, to know what parts of the proposal to stress, to know what loopholes you can slip into the bid to protect yourself in case you do win.

Work All Angles of a Support Contract to Line up Future Business.
Service work often is a marvelous surveillance post for future agency needs, upcoming bids, or expected funding levels. Contractor personnel are working closely with agency staffs, often on a daily basis. Few other avenues offer as good a chance to build inside relationships to parlay into future business. In the commercial market, company service personnel are trained to report back sales prospects and push company products. The need is even greater to tap service personnel for extra help in selling to Uncle Sam, and the payoff can be infinitely greater.

Service contractors are in a good spot to play the sole-source game. An adept contractor may be able to sell the buyer on special test equipment, on adding big training programs, or on expanding the scope of work of the contract. One adroit computer firm started with an unsolicited proposal for $30,000 to give data-processing service to a military hospital project and parlayed the contract into $3 million of funding.

> *Counterploy:* Competitors must have good agency intelligence to head off such sole-source expansions of service support contracts. By the time a buyer has revised a service contract upward, it's too late to salvage any chance for business. An appeal to agency superiors, pressure from Congress members, or alerting such supervisory agencies as the General Services Administration may stop such sole-source expansions and force agencies to seek competitive bids for the extra work.

Some Service Contracts Continue Year after Year. Agencies that are under no pressure to make any changes would rather stick with a known contractor than risk a competitive bid bringing in an unknown vendor. A good buyer can find suitable justification for extending service pacts to the same firm year after year—national security, urgent need, or the incumbent is the only firm with sufficient knowledge to handle the job. Even if forced to come out for bids, an agency can wire the competition for the incumbent firm by a bid deadline that is too short or by requiring special features only the existing contractor can provide. The task of any incumbent contractor is to play on the agency's fear of change to make sure that follow-on service contracts will come to it.

> *Counterploy:* Rivals must force lower-level officials to solicit bids for future service work by convincing agency superiors they can give a cheaper price and more effective support. Sometimes an unsolicited proposal to take over the service work will force agencies to come out with a competitive bid.

YOUR CHIEF COMPETITOR: UNCLE SAM

Service contractors soon learn that industry rivals may be the least of their problems. The biggest competitor is the in-house service work by government staffs.

The White House budget office estimates that there are 100,000 different in-house service activities within the federal government. Certainly bureaucracy must keep some in-house support capability: (1) It gives an agency enough expertise to judge contractor work, proposals, and cost estimates. No agency wants to be left solely at the mercy of contractors for its knowledge. (2) It gives an alternative source of support. Military services especially want to keep a strong in-house capability to react quickly to emergencies.

An unspoken reason for greater in-house work, however, is empire building. A project office can pyramid its size—and budget—by taking over more in-house service work itself. Conversely, in days of tight budgets, an agency can hold its empire intact by replacing outside contractor services by in-house support work.

Official U.S. government policy since 1966, however, has been to force agencies to use industry service support contractors rather than do work in-house. Known as Budget Circular A-76, this much-amended White House directive has failed to stem the growth of in-house service at the expense of industry. No ironclad directive can be written without some loopholes, and agencies are masters at justifying in-house work through the loopholes in Circular A-76.

Clever buyers can manipulate cost calculations to show that in-house work would be less costly than an outside contractor. These estimates may ignore many large parts of the in-house expense—insurance, warehousing, transportation, training, spare parts, depreciation of equipment used. But in most cases there is little challenge of the government estimate. If questioned, agencies can resort to their favorite diversionary tactic, making calculations so complex that no one really knows what they mean.

As a last resort, large in-house operations can mount a strong political campaign in Congress to head off shift of work to industry service contracts. Government workers at a large Navy base in California brought enough pressure on that state's representative in Congress to block large support contracts going to industry.

The only answer is your own political pressure through Congress to demand a true accounting of in-house costs, a continual banging away to shame government into honoring Circular A-76.

20

SOMETHING'S GOT TO BE DONE
The Odds on Changing the System

20. SOMETHING'S GOT TO BE DONE
The Odds on Changing the System

Sooner or later, anyone connected with government procurement reaches the exasperation point and wants to reform the System. The illogic, waste, unfairness, and inefficiency that pervade so much of federal buying is too much to bear. It is not just business people who hit the reform button. Retired government procurement officials, or even those still within the System, get fed up and call for a change. Members of Congress, the legal and accounting professions, the press—sometimes even a few irate citizens—get into the reform act.

Yet, just as surely as the cry for reform goes on, there is an equal certainty that little ever gets accomplished. The reasons are not hard to find. The previous chapters have outlined the vagaries of human nature, both of contractors and government buyers, that permeate the procurement process. Parkinson's Law has probably worked almost as long as Newton's.

Just as the state of technology has advanced, the state of buyocracy has progressed. New techniques, novel structures, and innovative strategies protect buyocrats more and more against change.

But beyond sheer bureaucratic inertia and obstinacy, reform movements go nowhere because:

1. Complex Problems, Such as Procurement Evils, Get Simplistic Solutions. Politicians, both in Congress and the Administration, don't have the energy or expertise to untangle complicated procurement problems. They look for the easy way out, the instant remedy pill. Officials at the top of the government hierarchy are buried under so many crises that they must shift problems into the out basket as fast as possible with quick and simple remedies. Because they don't have time to delve deeply into problems, they must suggest simplistic solutions for fear of proposing harmful remedies they don't fully understand.

Simplistic remedies are also forced by the warring factions around a procurement problem. Most such issues are made up of tangled shades of gray, but feuding factions often force their own extreme views, casting the issue into black and white.

These simple solutions are the easiest to circumvent because they rarely get to the root of a procurement disease, allowing bureaucratic ineptitude, waste, and bias to spread; allowing contractors to ply marketing tricks uncontested; and jeopardizing the very competitive procurement system that all claim must be preserved.

2. Logic Does Not Prevail in Procurement Reform. The more illogical a solution, the more likely the government is to adopt it. Industry often works by illogic also, but sooner or later the bottom profit line catches up with firms that drift too far out of the real world.

There is no bottom line in government, however. Thus, there are few checks against illogical solutions being implemented on procurement reforms.

Industry executives often mistakenly feel that their cause will prevail simply because it is right and just. They are increasingly shocked to find that government officials, looking through narrow glasses of self-interest, fail to see the sound logic of the situation.

Company officials are amazed to find high government leaders who have previously espoused the same principles as industry suddenly take an opposite course. The reason is inherent in the political process: the government official has political obligations throughout Congress and the Administration. Someone has called in a favor, forcing an abrupt about-face. Like the weather, public positions by government leaders are very changeable.

3. Uncle Sam Is Prosecutor, Judge, and Jury in All Procurement Reform Cases. The government is usually the source for most data and information. By structuring what material is presented, Uncle Sam can channel the decision process in the desired direction.

Reformers cannot press too hard for fear of antagonizing the only customer in the marketplace. Company executives often must state their cases in the weakest possible manner, making any meaningful procurement change unlikely right from the beginning.

Contractors frequently have different strategies in trying to bring reform, so industry often does not confront Uncle Sam with a united position. Clever bureaucrats can often win simply by divide and conquer tactics, scaring away a large contingent of contractors by implied retaliation.

Until some of these root causes of reform paralysis are attacked, there is little hope for change, no matter how many blue-ribbon panels or task forces are named.

With the odds stacked so heavily against change, is any attempt to improve the procurement system doomed? Realistically, reformers should not expect miracles. Rather, the same driving forces that impel both contractor and bureaucrat to short-circuit the system can be harnessed to improve it.

Some of the more obvious ways to bring about improvement are:

1. Reward Efficiency, Not Waste. It may seem axiomatic to promote the procurement official who does the best job. Indeed, the party line touts this image. But as we have seen, the real-world system too often does just the opposite. The program offices that do the worst job, run up the highest costs, and are the most inept are the very ones rewarded. The bigger the program costs, the larger a program office staff grows to shuffle the paperwork, monitor the contractor, and direct the project. No matter that agency or contractor waste are at fault. Both usually can cover their tracks with program changes, urgent new requirements, project redirection, national security secrecy, disguised new funding for spare parts or added work tasks, or any of a hundred different alibis that few overseers in government can challenge. One of the chief games buyocrats play is "build my empire," and runaway program costs, massive project changes, and heavy auditing of contractors are among the best ways to play the empire game. Any casual observer can prove this maxim: pick any bloated staff government program; the odds are it has one of the fastest increasing costs of any project. The worse you do, the bigger you grow.

The staggering maze of procurement regulations and directives promulgated almost daily make the situation worse. Almost every new regulation spawns a clutch of new bureaucrats to implement and monitor the directive, running costs up even higher.

Obviously, the answer is to reverse gears: reward agencies and project officials that bring in projects at target cost and on schedule. Salary or bonuses, the typical industry management carrots, are out. Civil Service forces the same pay scale on everyone in government, no matter how good or bad. But an even more effective motivation is at hand: let efficient, cost-saving bureaucrats expand their empire at the expense of wasteful, inept compatriots—the more trouble a project has, the *less* staff it gets.

A program office that meets target cost, schedule, and performance goals should be allowed to gradually take over expanded projects from less capable offices. Cautious expansion is the key. Otherwise, an effective, well-managed program office can become just as bloated and out of hand. There is just as great a danger that this bonus empire building can become as top-heavy and wasteful as conventional runaway buyocracy. This system must also be carefully monitored by agency superiors because staffers are sure to use contract gamesmanship to disguise cost increases and performance losses to make them look like successes.

Even if bonus empire building is not used, Uncle Sam can at least start penalizing the worst offenders for cost overruns, performance failures, and year-late deliveries. Instead of allowing project offices to grow to fill all available cost overrun, top agency budget offices should keep a tight lid on project staff funding. If errant program offices knew they would have to work twice as hard to make up for past mistakes, they would be more motivated to do the job right in the first place.

2. Controlled Interagency Rivalry Is Not Necessarily Wasteful. Competition may bring better procurements. Prevailing wisdom censures interagency rivalry. Indeed, the feuding between agencies, or even between different branches of the same agency, often leads to needless duplication, sending funding down the drain. Often agencies prefer to reinvent the wheel rather than accept a proven product or service developed by a rival agency.

Interagency rivalry is as close as government gets to the competitive commercial marketplace with its advantages. It may be the only time program offices are as motivated as their industry counterparts to bring in a superior product at the lowest cost. For the same reasons that commercial competition has been so successful, contending agencies want their project to win out—to advance careers and make the boss look good.

Limited competition between agencies to develop a new product or service should be fostered. Agency superiors, superagencies, and Congress could then select the best product. Perhaps Uncle Sam could benefit by continuing competition throughout the program life. Even if the government could not afford to buy two competing products, particularly on million-dollar projects, a competing agency could be funded to keep a rival product in development as a backstop to the product being bought.

3. Don't Get Caught Up in Minor Details. Uncle Sam has built up a mass of regulations for every minute buying evil. Name a minor misstep; there's a procurement directive against it—probably two or three directives at least, and they may be contradictory.

One would expect that such a saturation of rules and regulations would not allow a single miscue to occur. Far from it. The more microscopic the directives, the greater the procurement abuses. This should not be surprising. With tens of thousands of directives on every conceivable and even some inconceivable procurement actions, government overseers are so busy on minor infractions that buying outrages can slip by unchecked.

The more procurement directives that are issued, the more loopholes are created for abuses. No edict can be ironclad; every one must allow some exceptions for flexibility. Good buyocrats can spot a half dozen loopholes in even the most legally binding directive, and each directive drawn up to close these loopholes creates half a dozen more. In government, loopholes don't just multiply; they increase geometrically.

To many in industry the remedy is clear: don't try to pass a directive to cover every possible foible of human nature. Concentrate instead on the major buying abuses.

4. Enforce Buying Regulations Already on the Books; Don't Invent New Ones. There are already more than enough directives, rules, and edicts on the books to cover almost every procurement situation. If anything, some of the conflicting and contradictory regulations need to be weeded out.

A look at the books shows that the older the regulation, the more clearly is its obvious purpose stated. Only when agencies try to expand rules to cover every possible situation does a patchwork of confusion engulf everyone. Agency front offices, auditors, Congress, and White House overseers should concentrate on these obvious regulations and enforce the spirit of the law instead of writing new "letters of the law" to be evaded.

Of course, enforcement is far harder than making a big show of writing up a flurry of directives. Perhaps it can be encouraged by interagency rivalries or the desire of new employees to make names for themselves.

5. *When All Else Fails, Turn to Competition.* Directives mandating competition in procurement abound in government. By law, competitive advertised bidding is the preferred method of buying, but, as we've seen, competition gets a lot of lip service and still is too readily sidetracked or simply ignored.

There is a reason why competition is important in all the procurement codes. It offers the most flexibility, the greatest motivation for buyers and industry bidders, and the surest test of any procurement course. The General Accounting Office has consistently argued that programs acquired under competitive bid are far less costly than similar projects bought sole-source from favored vendors.

Buyers should not conduct a single competition and drop it for all future procurements. High-risk projects being developed for the first time should be carried in competition even through initial production orders. This way, an agency can motivate two or more competitive contractors through complex product development. If one firm bombs out, the agency has the backup competitor to carry on.

Buyers know this, but in the day-to-day rat race, lured by fanciful marketing visions spun by favorite vendors, project officials justify sole-source or restricted acquisitions. Too often project officers and their agency superiors are unwilling to spend the extra money needed to keep two or more contenders in a competition. They justify the expediency of going to a single vendor because they have limited funds or can't afford the extra time needed for competition. In the end, the agency usually ends up paying more in hidden costs, project bail-outs, and higher prices from the sole-source vendor that knows it's in the driver's seat.

No matter how many directives are issued mandating competitive bids, competition will not win out unless certain things happen.

Agency superiors or superagency authorities must crack down to make competitive edicts stick. Only if the boss is bent on competition will the working staff follow this course, which makes more initial work for them.

Effectiveness and cost saving must be rewarded and waste and cost overruns penalized. Nothing will spur interest in the benefits of competition more than being judged by actual performance, not alibis.

Vendors must stop playing a double standard, pressing for competitive bids on other vendors' projects but pushing for sole-source on their own. Industry's hypocrisy helps erode any strong support behind competitive procurement.

Competition is no cure-all. Competitive bids can be abused by buyers and vendors alike, as we have seen. Competition means buyers must draft precise and fair bid documents, select a winner with wisdom, and ride herd on contract performance. It forces contenders to make far greater effort, increases risks and uncertainties, and runs up company expenses as well as Uncle Sam's costs.

However, properly handled—and that is an important condition—fair competition generally is the best procurement method Uncle Sam has found. It at least puts some measurable yardstick to government buying, usually far better than contrived justifications of buyocrats for sole-source or restrictive procurements. There are countless ways that the competitive process will be uneven. There will be gains and losses. But every procurement reform panel ever set up by the government has concluded that competition, despite its many procurement problems, offers the best, and perhaps the only, way to achieve creditable government buying.

In the end, federal procurement is a business deal, a legal handshake between buyer (the biggest buyer in the world) and a seller. Stripped of all its complexities, bureaucratic strategies, and confusion, a government contract still depends on the good will and faith of the two parties to make it work. Often, when red tape, bureaucratic overkill, and political gyrations threaten to sink a contract, it is only the good faith of either party, or both, that salvages the project at all.

When runaway bureaucracy, vendor conniving, or legal gamesmanship threaten to overpower the normal business relationships routinely expected in the commercial marketplace, these perils must be attacked. Ill-conceived procurement practices, no matter how politically attractive, destroy the confidence of buyer and seller.

In spite of the problems, the U.S. procurement system is one of the best in the world—if not the best. The wholesale bribery, graft, and feudal nepotism so common in much of the world are isolated incidents here. Federal procurement may not be all that government officials claim, but it is a great deal better than buying procedures in other countries. When the system works, it is beautiful.

The goal of contractors and government officials alike must be to make it work, for the benefit of everyone. It can be done.

GLOSSARY OF COMMON ACRONYMS

ARS   Advanced Records System, the civilian interagency national data transmission network

ASPR   Armed Services Procurement Regulations, now called Defense Acquisition Regulations System (DARS), 3000 pages on everything you wanted to know about DOD buying policies

BOA   Buying Order Agreement, a blanket open-to-buy contract with a vendor, supposedly for small purchases but suspected by many to be abused for sole-source purchases

CAS   Cost Accounting Standards, Uncle Sam dictating how you will keep your financial books if you have negotiated contracts of any nominal size

CBD   *Commerce Business Daily,* a daily tip sheet on government bids printed by the Commerce Department, valuable if you know how to use it

CFR   Code of Federal Regulations, the legal bible governing all government operations; Volume 41, *Public Contracts and Property Management,* covers most procurement rules and is surprisingly readable

CO   Contracting Officer, the only legal authority for the government on a contract (what any other project staffer says has no legal standing); usually the CO is one identifiable person, but often on large contracts the CO is a contingent of agency officials, and the CO's name on the contract is only the legal front for this group

COC   Certificate of Competence, a verification by the Small Business Administration that an apparent small company winner on a bid can perform the work on the contract; legally binding on agencies

CP   Cost-Plus Contract, Uncle Sam agrees to pick up the tab for contract costs; not a blank check, since agencies tightly control allowable costs

CPAF   Cost-Plus Award Fee Contract, the same as CPIF, except here the bonus fee is not specified in the contract but is left entirely to the discretion of the CO

CPIF   Cost-Plus Incentive Fee Contract, a cost-reimbursal contract with a carrot: the extra bonus fee paid to vendor for meeting or surpassing target goals

DARS   Defense Acquisition Regulation System, the new name for ASPR; all the old rules plus some new ones

D&F   Determination and Finding, in the Department of Defense this is the legal justification for a sole source, an RFP, or other type of negotiated award (called Finding and Determination in civilian agencies)

DPA   Delegation of Procurement Authority, one agency shifts the procurement action to another agency or to another office within the same agency; this often results in disputes over just what procurement authority was delegated

DPC   Defense Procurement Circular, consisting of newly adopted rules to be included in the appropriate sections of DARS (originally ASPR) in the next annual printing

FAR   Federal Acquisition Regulations, a proposed single, unified body of procurement rules to cover both civilian agencies and the Department of Defense; this mammoth undertaking has an early 1980s target date for completion

F&D   Finding and Determination, the civilian agency version of the Department of Defense's D&F

FP   Fixed-Price Contract, Uncle Sam pays only the agreed contract price; you absorb any costs above this price

FPAF   Fixed-Price Award Fee, the same type of contract as FP, with a possible bonus for meeting or exceeding target goals, given at the discretion of the CO

FPIF   Fixed-Price Incentive Fee, the same type of contract as FP, with a possible bonus, not at the discretion of the CO

FPR   Federal Procurement Regulations, all the buying rules for civilian agencies, comparable to the Department of Defense's DARS or ASPR

FSS   Federal Supply Service or Federal Supply Schedule, blanket open-to-buy contracts negotiated with vendors by the General Services Administration and against which agencies can place limited orders; a favorite sole-source method

GAO   General Accounting Office, the government auditor, an arm of Congress; handles contractor protests and has even been known to uphold a few protests

GFE   Government-Furnished Equipment, any material, components, subsystems, tooling, or test equipment supplied by an agency directly to the contractor; sometimes arrives late, is deficient, and causes a flurry of claims

GOCO   Government Owned, Contractor Operated, usually a plant owned by Uncle Sam that is run by a prime contractor

GSA   General Services Administration, the government quartermaster, keeping an inventory of more than 4 million different items

IFB   Invitation for Bid, the common straight advertised bid with low-price bidder automatically the winner

IR&D   Independent Research and Development. The Department of Defense and some other agencies help foot the cost of company's purely exploratory research under the theory that unplanned spinoffs from this work find their way into government projects. Usually funded as a small percentage of total annual contractor business with the government and negotiated as an agreement just as any contract. You must ask for an IR&D agreement—agencies won't automatically give it to you. Usually restricted to research and development contractors.

MIL-spec   Military Specification, every one of more than 30,000 DOD specifications, each numbered (e.g., MIL-S-1633); hundreds of MIL-specs may be called out in a defense bid

MOL   Maximum Order Limitation, most commonly used with GSA Federal Supply Schedule contracts to set the dollar value or quantity limits of any purchase

NIH   Not Invented Here, a slang term of federal officials and contractors denoting the reluctance of agencies to accept concepts or products they have not thought of themselves; often the reason why government buyers will not beat a path to the door of a firm with a better mousetrap

OMB   Office of Management and Budget, the White House budgeters, who are over all federal agencies; this office also coordinates procurement policies through the Office of Federal Procurement Policy (OFPP)

QPL   Qualified Products List, a "blue book" list of products previously tested by an agency and qualified for future purchases

RFI   Request for Information, an agency invitation for vendors to supply detailed product data and systems design at their own expense; a freebie for Uncle Sam

RFP   Request for Proposal, a negotiated procurement constituting the bulk of government purchases and what most of this book is all about

RFQ   Request for Quotation, a limited form of negotiated procurement for smaller dollar amount purchases

INDEX